WORKING MOTHERS 101

WORKING MOTHERS

101

HOW TO ORGANIZE YOUR LIFE, YOUR CHILDREN, AND YOUR CAREER TO STOP FEELING GUILTY AND START ENJOYING IT ALL

KATHERINE WYSE GOLDMAN

Cliff Street Books
An Imprint of HarperCollinsPublishers

HarperCollins books may be purchased for educational, business, or sales promotional use. For information please write: Special Markets Department, HarperCollins Publishers, Inc., 10 East 53rd Street, New York, NY 10022.

FIRST EDITION

Designed by Laura Lindgren

Library of Congress Cataloging-in-Publication Data

Goldman, Katherine Wyse.
    Working mothers 101 : how to organize your life, your children, and your career to stop feeling guilty and start enjoying it all / Katherine Wyse Goldman. — 1st ed.
        p. cm.
    ISBN 0-06-095237-7
    1. Working mothers — Time management — United States. I. Title.
HQ759.48.G65 1998
646.7'0085'2—dc21   98-6530

---

01 02 ❖ / RRD   10 9 8 7 6 5 4

For Tessie, who taught me more than she'll ever know.
(On second thought, wherever she is, she probably does.)

CONTENTS

ACKNOWLEDGMENTS

One thing about being a working mother, you're eternally grateful to all the special people who help you get your work done. I'm no exception. For their ideas, brainstorms, shoulders, ears and general all-around help, I offer my thanks to my editors Diane Reverand and Meaghan Dowling at HarperCollins; to agents Jane Dystel and Miriam Goderich; to good friends Helene Silver, Sharyn Rosenblum, Nancy Kelley, Wendy Ruther, Martha Kaplan, Alix Barthelmes, Amy Krakow, and Monica Bernstein; to the Philadelphia book group, the City & Company gang, and Mom.

Thanks, too, to all the generous mothers who inked me in and shared their wonderful words, thoughts, and benefits of their hard work.

And, of course, I couldn't do a thing without my family. Thanks to Henry, Max, and Molly, who deliver love and support with their special charm and grace. (Thanks for the cake, guys.) I'm proud to call them my own.

> "We're all smart women.
> If there were one way to do this,
> we'd all be doing it."

INTRODUCTION

Why You Need Another Book About Motherhood

Baby and Child Care? Yep.

What to Expect When You're Expecting? Certainly.

Your Baby & Child? It's there.

Okay, you have them. You made sure they were on the shelf before you were a mother. But now that you are—now that you're a *working* mother—are you finding what you need between the covers?

Is there a rundown of carpooling, packing for camp, cleaning your house, making Thanksgiving dinner, interviewing a prospective sitter, filling out your family calendar, shopping at the supermarket, finding a good plumber, meeting your child's new teacher, and planning a vacation . . . all while holding a full-time job?

Not exactly.

Here's a book about you. About your child, to be sure, but first about you. With the number of chores, duties and responsibilities that you have, you can often feel that you don't get anything done or you don't get the right things done, that the tiny details—which are still eminently important—overshadow the big things. You might even wake up in the middle of the night worrying about what you didn't do. Your life feels out of control, that you can't even tell anyone where to begin to pitch in. You're exhausted, overwhelmed, and mess up simple tasks.

You've come to the right place for help.

Now that your life is inflated with children who are filling up their lives and their rooms with who they are, you want to downsize your life. Simplify it. Make it easier, more organized, less complicated.

In these pages you'll find answers. You won't learn how to be Supermom. After all, I'm merely a working mother, just like you. I'm not talking to you as a sociologist, psychologist, pediatrician, or organizational expert, although I'm not too bad at any of these. I'm a Doctor of Thinkology like the scarecrow in *The Wizard of Oz*. I can figure out a few things, and if I don't know the answer, I know enough to ask. To find more strategies and tips for you, I went to our greatest resource: other working mothers.

And just because I say you can get organized doesn't mean I believe, insist, or even faintly imagine that you can do it all. Your life is already crammed with compromises. There's not a chance you can do everything and be everything, and you should not feel guilty about it.

This is a book to help you take a deep breath and categorize your life. It will help you put things in order and check off things you've done. But as much practical stuff there is to do every single day, always remember that we're talking about bloodlines, not bottom lines. Find the joy in your family, your career, and the world around you.

We're fortunate to live in a society that is acknowledging our responsibilities as well as our need to raise our children to be the best people they can be. Finally, we can keep pictures of our children on our desks, leave early to get to a Little League game, ask to work from home if a daughter is sick, or take a son's call during a meeting to help him with his homework.

Never forget who you are. Always be proud to walk into a meeting and say, "Hello, my name is Mom."

WORKING MOTHERS 101

> *"I have no time to make time."*

∷ 1 ∷

The Secret to a Less Stressed Life: *Get Organized*

I know you don't have a lot of time, so let's get right to the point.

Organization Is the Key to Your Life

Oh, no, here's somebody else telling you how to live your life to be the perfect mother-worker-wife. Fear not. I live far from the world of perfection, and I not only can't draw you a road map to get there, but I'm sure a few of the bridges are out.

We All Think We Have to Do It

Go into any office tomorrow morning, at any level, and you'll hear the women who are talking about potty training, pediatricians, day camp versus sleep away, and making brownies at midnight. How many working mothers do you know who say that all they want is a wife?

The real reason we take it all on? We still see ourselves as good little girls. Would any daughter of a certain age sit at the dinner table and watch her mother clear and do the dishes? Don't you make coffee and clean up the dirty mugs at the office?

WE HAVE A VISION OF HOW IT SHOULD BE

Louise is a bank executive specializing in risk management, but she has the good little girl still operating in her brain. When she was given a forty-page document to distill into a two-page report, she worked on it immediately. When her boss called to ask whether she'd even had a chance to look at the original document, she looked at the finished report sitting on her desk.

We also notice certain things that indicate whether we are managing the home scene well. Jane, a marketing executive, left for a business trip early one Tuesday morning before her two young children were up. When she returned home Wednesday, she saw that her children had been dressed again in the same clothes she'd put them in on Monday. "Don't you think someone would realize it?" she wondered. A mother would.

We Better Be Doing the Home Job
Very, Very Well First

We are still struck with this idea of expectations: our job—our *real* job—is to manage the home and family. And even though boys are beginning to understand that they too live in a world that's full of varied responsibilities, we know that if we want to have that other outside job, we have to become juggling masters.

Mothers Aren't Surprised to Learn Any of This

The only surprise is that we've grown to like what we do outside the home, that there's something rewarding about having responsibilities and making money, and that we want all the experiences life has to offer us.

If we want it, we better get organized.

Time Is Really the Problem

You're going to have to find ways to put more space in your day and to make more of it available for the people and activities that you've decided are most important to you.

Have a Plan

There's too much going on to keep it all in your head.

- Get an organizer. Any organizer. No matter what kind you use, from good old-fashioned paper to a sophisticated, patented system you were taught at the office, to software you installed on your laptop, be in charge of it.
- Live by lists. Keep the Mother of All Lists. Hidden between the lines on our lists to pick up the dry cleaning and buy more juice boxes are unwritten reminders to save for college, teach values, and get those college applications in on time, even if we're the mothers of newborns. We have the whole twenty-five years in mind from day one.

Begin with the Organizing Principle: Prioritizing

No mother has ever regretted on her deathbed that she didn't spend enough time at the office.

- Put your life into perspective.
- Spend a few minutes right now—not before every event of every day—deciding what is important. You'll be able to make decisions about how to use your time much more easily.
- Don't just say it. Act on it.

KNOW WHAT YOU WANT

Shelly is the chief executive officer of a multinational company. Throughout her career she has known that her three children were most important to her.

"Three weeks after I was made a management supervisor," says Shelly, "a client called to say he wanted me to attend a five-day off-site meeting. I looked at my calendar and saw that my middle-school son had field day, which I promised to attend. I told the client I couldn't be at the meeting. 'You're kidding, right?' he asked. I told him, 'Three weeks from now you'll never remember who was at the meeting, but my son will never forget I wasn't at school.'"

Early in her career as a working mother, Shelly put this list together:

What I do:
- Clothes shopping
- Pediatrician
- Dentist
- Haircuts
- School plays
- School concerts
- Weekend dinners

- Birthday parties
- Homework

What I don't do:
- School cocktail parties
- Adult dinner parties on Saturday night
- The gym

What I miss:
- Browsing through stores

Her son told her recently that he always knew if there were any important event she'd be there. "True," she says. "And he said he knew that if he ever called me at the office, my secretary was always to find me. Not true, but I'm glad that he felt it."

What to Ask Yourself to Come Up with Your Priorities

- How ambitious am I?
- How many hours a week do I want to spend at the office?
- How many evenings a week am I willing to work late?
- Can I have the kind of career I want if I switch to a part-time schedule?
- How many of those business dinners do I really have to go to?
- Am I going to have a career left if I don't do any traveling?
- Am I willing to bring work home?
- What kind of help am I willing to get?
- Is my children's appearance every day important to me?
- Can I live in a less-than-spotless house?
- Do I have to shop for everybody's clothes?
- Do I want to know every single thing my children eat?
- Do I want to drive carpools?
- How active do I want to be in my children's school?

- How important are my friends to my well-being?
- What kind of relationship do I want to have with my husband?
- Do I trust anyone to take my children to the doctor?
- How much do I need to be involved in the community?
- Do I have to do holidays just as my mother did?
- What can I give up to have the kind of career and family life I want?

There are always questions of agonizing guilt popping into your mind. This might be a good time to start a journal. Jot things down in a little notebook; don't write great tomes. Keep track of what you're thinking about.

Know the Kind of Person You Want to Be

Remember the kind of values and goals you developed when you were young and idealistic.

Goals that might have gotten lost behind the refrigerator:
- To be honorable
- To be someone who won't shortchange a recipient
- To be someone to whom people (such as children, husband, colleagues) can come for guidance

YOU CAN DO IT ALL . . . EVENTUALLY

Even if you wish you could help out in your community, have every intention of doing it, and feel horrendously guilty every time you turn down an organization that asks you to volunteer, forget it. Everything happens in time.

Kathy is an interior architect who adapts her schedule to clients who need to see her at their own crazy hours. What's more, she decided that she couldn't survive without having a social life—a private one with her husband and a rousing one with other families—

and teaching Sunday school. She knows which invitations to turn down. "I'm not Supermom," she says. "I don't have time for all the charities I'd like to help. But I will do it when the kids are older. I plan on doing it all."

Set Up a Life You Can Actually Live

- Have one calendar called Command Central. Blocks should be big enough so you can write down enough information.
- Make sure your calendar lets you see a year at a time.
- Give up organization by Post-its. Ever notice how they lose their stickiness? Take that as a sign.
- Keep your own personal calendar, too, that's always with you.

A FAMILY NEEDS GOALS

If you have to meet quarterly projections at work, why not apply it to the home front? Have family goals, too, and write them down every three months.

Your goals could include having your kids signed up for piano lessons, taking a vacation, or selecting your child's preschool. Set the goals, then work backwards to make sure they're done. How do you get them accomplished? Call friends to find a piano teacher, get brochures from a travel agent, and locate the best child-care facility near your office.

What Goes on the Family Calendar

- Every single school event
- Anything special you have to send along with your child to school that day, from money to cups and juice for a party
- Changes such as a special bag lunch, a different pick-up time, or a change in your usual getting-home arrangements
- After-school activities and programs
- Parent-teacher meetings
- Who's baby-sitting
- Your business trip, a business dinner, or social engagements that are going to impact the life of the family
- Birthday parties, with all the details about who, where, the phone number, and how your child is getting there. Invitations stuck to the refrigerator are not surefire reminders.
- Sports practices, sports events, and any changes.
- Lessons, performances of music or drama, and the ever-popular school play
- Everything you possibly know about camp

    For day camp, write first and last days plus any special days you may know about so that you are not looking for a costume, aluminum pie plates, and a clean white T-shirt fifteen minutes before the children have to leave in the morning.

    For sleep-away camp, forget the whole calendar. Take a vacation. But highlight the date you have to send the goodie packages.
- Holiday stuff, family events, Grandma's visit
- Vacations and how child care is being handled
- Medical appointments

TIP FOR PRESCHOOLERS

Note on your Family Calendar things like the letter of the week or any other pertinent information the teacher sends home about what's going on in school. It helps you stay connected with a small person who may not be able to articulate exactly what's going on.

What's on Your Personal Calendar?

Besides your diminished personal life and bloated work schedule, put these in your datebook:
- The school schedule.
- Any nighttime meetings.
- Any regularly scheduled lessons and appointments.
- Kids' medical appointments and haircuts.
- Every school event for which you've volunteered.
- Transfer anything from the family calendar that disrupts your usual schedule so that you don't miss it.
- If your schedule is on a computer or a personal digital assistant, back it up. Hard drives die; you'll lose every date, every phone number, every address.

CARPOOL TIPS

Whenever you coordinate a carpool, or if you take your children to a school-bus stop, volunteer to collect all the names, addresses, and phone numbers, then enter the data in your computer and print out a list for everybody.

Include a schedule of driving responsibilities, if applicable. Obviously, not every working mother can drive a regular schedule. If parents (and sitters, nannies, or au pairs) change their schedule, have them call one another to coordinate. Once you've done the initial compilation, step out of it. You don't have the time.

Live by the Numbers

No date book is efficient if it doesn't qualify as the one possession you'd grab as you run out of a burning building. You need a lifeline to important people.

Keep these numbers in your datebook:
- Social security numbers of your family
- Frequent flyer numbers of your family so you can book a flight anytime
- Phone numbers of alternative sitters
- Phone numbers of your children's doctors so you can make appointments when you think of it
- Phone numbers of pharmacies near work and home
- School phone and fax
- The number of someone you could call to pick your children up in an emergency

TAKE TIME TO MAKE TIME

Get in the habit of inputting schedule information into your calendar the minute you hear about it. Empty your children's book bags, which will have notices that are going to be your only communication about events and calendars. Write down vacation dates, business trips, parties, doctors' appointments, school meetings. It helps you plan for sitters, meals, and carpools as well as prepare young children for events and changes that are imminent.

Being on top of the schedule is exactly what a good secretary does. And, face it, you're the family secretary.

Keep All the Important Information
Near Your Family Calendar

You have to live on automatic pilot, and you can't be the only one who knows all the important data like the plumber's number. Put it in your computer, store it on your hard drive, and print out a list for the kitchen. Make sure everybody knows where it is.

- Emergency contacts
- Doctors' and pharmacy numbers and addresses
- Health insurance information
- School/Day-care phone
- The class phone list
- Numbers for plumber, electrician, roofer, snow removal, tree surgeon, alarm company, exterminator, handyman, heating and air-conditioning service, pizza delivery

---

TIP FOR MIDDLE SCHOOLERS

You don't get that nice class list anymore. In fact, you probably don't get half the information you used to get. So do yourself a favor and get the phone numbers of your child's friends. You are going to have to reach your child, you know. Try to update this list frequently. And, if possible, get the names of parents.

The First Principle of Non-Supermom Is Asking for Help

You really don't have to do this alone. Other people live in the house with you, and they can take some responsibility for making the house run smoothly. All right, somewhat smoothly.

When you have a baby, it's between you and your partner to work out the responsibilities. When you ask for help, make it clear that this is a partnership, not a monarchy.

- Divide up responsibilities; don't mete out chores.
- You're both permitted to set standards of excellence.
- Don't make your husband feel he's helping you out. Women won't be able to stop feeling angry about men's not helping until women stop thanking men for doing

stuff they should be doing anyway. Does anybody thank you for emptying the dishwasher or picking up the children?

WHAT DID SHE EXPECT?

Gene was making the bed with her husband one morning, as they had done together every morning for a zillion years, when one of her children asked her to help find a sneaker. Gene left, and when she came back, her husband was standing at the bed, which was at the same stage of undress. "Why didn't you finish?" she asked.

"I was waiting for you to come back so I could help you finish," he replied.

"You are not helping me make the bed," she told him. "We are making our bed together." She never in all those years knew that he hadn't understood that.

HOW TO GET A HUSBAND TO HELP

- Tell him exactly what you want him to do. He doesn't want to disappoint you.
- Let him know why you want help. Say to him, for example, "Have you ever had to worry when you open the diaper bag that diapers or wipes or a change of clothes won't be in it? I make it easy for you, and I want you to make it easy for me."
- Say something like, "Can you throw in a load of whites when the washer has finished?" Be sure you've already shown him how to use the washer.
- Understand that he probably didn't grow up with a father who wanted to help as much as he does.
- Give him his own territory such as Little League or day-care drop-off, in which he can establish his own relationships.
- If he has a regular schedule and yours is crazy, have him pick up the kids and do dinner.

- Accept the man you've got. He probably can't iron, and he won't wipe the kitchen counters exactly as you would.
- Know when to give up. You just might be picking up his socks or packing lunches for the children for the rest of your life yourself.

HAVE HIM DO WHAT HE'S GOOD AT

Angela is a human resources manager and admits freely that she is not good about keeping track of all of the stuff that comes home from school. But her husband, a lawyer, is much better about paying attention to detail. "He reads all of those notices that come home in the book bag and leaves me a list of something I have to do or get. It's a huge help, and it lets me be sloppy about remembering to look, which I would feel guilty not doing."

Who Helps When You Don't Have a Husband?

Are you sitting there reading about getting your husband to help and asking, "What husband?" There are resources when you're on your own.

- Get a buddy at work, one who can help with responsibilities if you have to get a report out (although you also have to stay home with a sick child).
- Talk with your company's human resources director or your supervisor about establishing an on-site support network. An employee-run group that meets once a week for a brown bag lunch can help one another with pressing issues.
- Actively seek carpools.
- Join a baby-sitting network.
- Take the help of everyone who offers it. Let friends take your child to the movies, to Little League, away for the weekend.

Learn to Turn to Resources Outside Your Home

Coupled or not, you have friends. Honestly. You might not see them much for social occasions anymore, but calling upon them is a good way to keep in touch while getting help. Many mothers turn to many places.

- Your mother. Even if she's in another city, call her up to vent.
- Assorted relatives who do live nearby. Call and ask. Sometimes your family is afraid you'll think they're criticizing or interfering.
- Local parenting papers. They will give you lots of information about resources in your community. The calendars, tips, and articles about schools, camps, and classes are invaluable for a mother who spends very little time standing outside the kindergarten room every morning talking to other mothers.
- Trust yourself. You have great instincts.

How to Give Back to Your Friends Who Help (and We're Not Talking Tiffany's)

- Give in kind.
- You don't have to build in any extra time for it.
- Give your friends' children something from your work (old magazines, markers, computer chips, wallpaper, or flooring samples for art projects).
- If you're running to the drugstore or convenience store, call and ask if you can pick something up for her.
- Have a buddy system with another working mother. If one of you is in a crunch at work, tell each other, then swap dinner duty during that time. Make easy dishes that serve a crowd, like spaghetti or lasagna and salad, and share the costs.

GET YOUR CHILD-REARING TIPS FROM THE EXPERTS: WOMEN WHO ARE LIVING THROUGH IT

When Ann had her first baby after forty, then went back to work immediately, she knew there was no author, expert, or doctor who could tell her what to do. "I talked to every working mother I met," she said. "I had always wondered why women were always talking about this stuff at parties, and now I knew. We're hungry for it."

Cyndi is a marketing director of a local bank and has two toddlers. "By the time I paid attention to my job and my kids, I had no identity anymore as a wife and absolutely none as a person. I lost myself somewhere in there."

She changed things to have more time. All her little tricks might save ten minutes here and there, but she's found it's made her whole life easier.

- She grew her hair longer and wears it in a ponytail.
- She changes into sweats or shorts and a T-shirt before leaving work so that she doesn't have to spend time changing when she gets home and her kids don't get dirty fingers on her suits.
- She leaves a supply of after-day-care snacks for her kids at work so she doesn't have to think about packing them up in the mornings.
- Her kids brush their teeth in the tub at night, which saves ten minutes plus time for wiping up the sink, and sleep in the sweats they'll wear to day care the next morning.
- She makes dinner and sets the dinner table the night before.

And now? "I feel I have time for everything," she says, "even to watch TV with my husband at night."

Are You Ready for Family Meetings?

Make the meetings a time when everybody finds out what's going on that week as well as a forum for airing concerns and complaints. Then leave a little time at the end to offer to talk one-on-one with anybody who needs it.

THE FAMILY MEETING AGENDA
- Keep it short. We're talking ten minutes. . . up to twenty.
- Go over the weekly calendar. Discuss who is participating in each event and how they are getting there.
- Once your children are old enough, give them their own calendars that they can bring to the meetings. They'll feel so responsible.
- Figure out if you need to buy anything for an event, such as a birthday present, costume, or soccer shoes.
- Determine whether you need to get any baby-sitting help.
- Hand out money for school trips, lunches, allowances.
- Talk about any school projects coming up so you don't have a hysterical child starting a research paper the night before it's due.

Line Your Day with Time Cushions

Life with children is anything but predictable. Cranky, moody, tired, hungry, anxious—no matter what age, they're all affected by mysterious and powerful forces.

Adapting to your tough schedule is a lot to ask of a kid. With all that pressure, kids need to bump into time cushions so they don't feel everything is on them.

Morning is a particularly bad time. There's no other time of the day when you use every single minute so carefully.
- Try getting up earlier.
- Shower and dress before you wake the children.
- Make sure there's gas in the car the night before.

- Pack all the your stuff and the kids' at night and load the car. If that's not possible, at least have it all by the door before you go to bed.

It never works if you're running around as much as they are.

A CASE FOR MORE MELLOW MORNINGS

Marion's middle-school son had built a suspension bridge out of balsa wood for a school project, and had worked hours and hours on it. The day they were taking it to school, Marion was in a rush to be at work early for an important meeting, her husband needed her to help him find socks and a shirt, and her two children were moving at a snail's pace.

She describes the morning: "I was yelling and stomping like a maniac to get them out of the house. We finally got in the car, and my son sat in the front with his bridge on the seat between us. When I got in, I didn't take the time to open the back door and place my purse and briefcase on the floor behind my seat. Instead, I threw them in the front seat on top of the bridge. I ruined it.

"We both burst into tears, and all I could think was, 'You wicked witch. Look how you treat your children.' It was the guiltiest moment I've had as a mother. He took it to school broken, I called the teacher, who let him fix it, and my son forgave me, probably because it wasn't his fault. All mine."

Time to Be

With all this scheduling, you might think there's no time to just be. Of course there is, though, naturally, you have to plan for it.

This is that weird segment of the day or week some have designated as "quality time," which always sounds to me like the time you're teaching a preschooler the rudiments of calculus. It's better described as a time that creates memories. What do you want your children to remember about growing up?

CREATE FAMILY RITUALS

- Don't make plans with other couples on Saturday night. Stay home, make dinner as a family, rent a movie, sleep on the family-room rug in your sleeping bags.
- Have a baking project on Saturday afternoon, and let the kids plan it. Remember, a brownie mix is also baking.
- When you can, try to have dinner as a family, even if the children have to wait for you to get home.
- Talk with each child separately at bedtime about how the day went.
- Read aloud to your children for as many years as they'll let you.
- Have a game that your family plays together—card game, board game, made-up game, or even charades. It's the kind of ritual that grows up with the children.
- King or queen for a day: on weekends or holidays, spend a day with your child who's planned everything from food to activities. Give a budget!
- Get your children involved in your work. If you bring one to the office, have him or her help in some way to see what you do all day.
- Make real plans for one day each weekend so that it doesn't just drift away with errands or running to birthday parties or events.

Lest you think that you are doing irreparable damage to your children, who will spend their lives shaking and running from room to room in the house, checking off endless lists on their personal electronic organizers or who will never be anywhere on time, live in impossible messes, and

never be able to hold a job or be in a meaningful relationship, relax.

Whatever it is, your children are going to accept their
active lives as normal. This is the life they are growing up
living. If you make them feel loved and cared for, the sense
that a rich, full life is normal will make them leaders and
doers who are satisfied people able to contribute to the
world around them.

▪▪ 2 ▪▪

File It, Find It, Clean It:
How to Create Order to Feel Comfortable at Home

The mess, the piles, and the dust bunnies probably burst into your life when your own cuddly bunny first arrived home from the hospital. During your maternity leave, you spent your days throwing in load after load of laundry, and practiced folding a stroller with one hand and packing the diaper bag in just three minutes. When were you supposed to tidy up a bit? Add a full-time job to that, and you put it off for years.

The time does come, though, when it all gets to be a bit much and you want to live like a relatively civilized person.

After all, this is what you are telling your children to do, and you have to set an example. ("If Mommy didn't clean off her desk every night, she wouldn't be able to find anything, dear.") I have found, though, that stepping on sharp little Happy Meal toys in the middle of the night is an extraordinary impelling force to finally find permanent homes for all of it.

That stuff begins to take over your life when you notice that no one ever comes through the door empty-handed.

Your children are just beginning to establish themselves, to learn their passions, find their own places in the world. You really have to indulge and respect all that precious matter they collect. My daughter used to bring home a book bag filled with diamonds that she and her friends dug up from the kindergarten playground every day. My son saves the ticket stub and program from every single play or sporting event he goes to. He's creating his history, which he can review many years from now. So what's a mother to do?

Start with Your Children's Rooms

You can't put it away if there's no away. Take a tip from preschool, and have a place for everything.

There, your kids are taught from day one to put things back where they belong. Give your children a sense of order very early. The kids should know that if the President of the United States were coming for dinner, they could actually clean their rooms without having to jam everything into the closets.

The basic rules of preschool organization apply:
• Build shelves at eye level and below
• Have a specific spot where each toy goes
• Leave a play space in the middle of the room
• Put each toy away before you take out the next one
• Have boxes for all the little pieces

- Group materials by purpose: all art stuff in one area, puzzles in one area, little cars in one area
- Impose the rule: clean up when you are finished, or you don't get a snack

Kids Have Two Categories to Organize: Clothes and Stuff

CLOTHES
- Use hooks for robes, jackets, hats (display them on a wall), jewelry, necklaces. Sew little tabs into items if they need them for hanging. Children (up through high school) aren't great with hangers. A closet filled with hooks makes kids much more likely to put their things away. Hooks also work well on the backs of doors or designated sections on a wall.
- Have a clothes hamper in your child's room. Didn't you know it's almost a mile to the bathroom?
- Invest in closet organizers to incorporate shelves, drawers, and hanging areas into one space.
- Put their out-of-season clothes out of sight so that they know what to wear.
- Don't keep their drawers too full. They won't be able to find anything.
- Label the drawers so they know what goes in them, and show them specifically.

STUFF
- Have plenty of open shelving.
- Two shelves (don't forget about the floor) for little kids; three shelves for older children.
- Get clear plastic boxes for little pieces so they know what's in the box.
- If you're a neatness freak, have tops for the boxes.
- Forget a big toy box. Everything they want is on the bottom.

- Have a rule for collections: if something new comes in, something old goes out.
- Toys do not come out of their rooms into the rest of the house.
- Rotate toys to keep the children interested. It seems like a whole new bunch every Saturday when they're pulled out.
- Hang a little hammock for stuffed animals from the ceiling, and make that their home.
- Put a clear plastic shoe bag on the back of the door for things from grooming items to little toys.

BOYS AND THEIR CARD COLLECTIONS

If you have a son of a certain age, he might have a huge collection that he wants to keep for a lifetime, and those are his sports cards. These cards that used to come with powdery flat bubble gum are now financing college educations, so it makes sense to take care of them. He has good intentions, but doesn't always follow through, which means that for a while, instead of being the old-fashioned mother who threw those things out, you will be the security guard. Here are tips on taking care of them:

- Put least valuable cards in shoe boxes.
- Put more valuable cards into binders with plastic pages. These are in the sports-card stores. You don't have to look far.
- Most valuable cards go into hard plastic cases, and these should go into some kind of indestructible box.
- Autographs and photos can go into large plastic sleeves that fit into binders.

Cleaning the Room

Consider the scene. You arrive home from work, go into your child's room to say hello, encounter a mess, feel powerless and guilty because you're not home cleaning it, so you start to scream. Change it.

- Clean only one part of it at a time.
- Start with the clothes on the floor, the socks under the bed.
- Another day, put the toys on the shelves.
- Put things away in alphabetical order with your child.
- Don't ask your child to do it alone. It won't happen.
- Clean it together. Admire it together.
- In two days, it will be a wreck.

WHAT TO DO WHEN YOUR KID CAN'T GET ORGANIZED

It used to be that we suffered through our children's inability to focus. We had no understanding of it, merely an intolerance for it. For many children, the diagnosis is Attention Deficit Disorder (ADD).

Andrea and her son both have ADD, and their need for organization is very important. "I have difficulty focusing, and I come by this honestly. My mother was completely disorganized and couldn't get out of the house. She would always need that one piece of paper that was buried under sixty thousand cat food coupons that expired in 1968. We used to joke that Jimmy Hoffa was buried in her apartment.

"My mother was an artist, and so am I. I was raised to believe that if you are an artist, you have a license to be confused and flaky. It doesn't work when you're a mother. I was very critical of myself, but then I learned to assess when too much is too much.

"Cleaning up was high on my list of priorities. When my son was diagnosed, I knew I had to help him be systematic. He was leaving his stuff all over the house,

---

and neither one of us could find it. To get serious, we labeled every box and every drawer in his room so he'd know where to put something—and where to find it later. Being very specific in how we organized his room and in how he keeps it in order has been a lifesaver."

Give the Children Responsibilities

Give your children specific duties so they understand that keeping things organized and neat is an ongoing aspect of life.

Get them involved in maintenance of the entire house, not just their own little domains. Try to instill it early.

To come up with a list of chores, write down all the things you would like to have done around your house. Then get the kids involved at an appropriate age. They're going to have their own homes eventually.

Here are some chores you can teach your kids to do:
- Set the table. Little ones start with place mats, and progress to napkins, flatware, dishes, and glasses
- Clear their own places from the table
- Empty the trash
- Sort cans, glass, and plastic for recycling
- Empty the dishwasher
- Put their own folded laundry away
- Make their beds
- Shovel snow
- Vacuum
- Pull weeds—point out which are the weeds
- Plant annuals—do this together
- Put the sprinkler out and turn it on
- Help wash the car
- Sweep around the outside doors

What to Do with the School Projects

They're big, unruly, don't store particularly well, but your little Picasso did them. Here's where they go:

- Get a big box at the beginning of every school year and label it. Include a photo from the first and last day of school so your children can see how they changed. Keep this in a storage area.
- Keep putting papers into the big box all year long. At the end of the school year, look through it with your child to edit further. It's amazing how much less interesting the spelling tests will look at the end of the year.
- For you art lovers, have your child choose two special papers a day (or weekly, if that's how they come home) to save. Put one on the refrigerator or a bulletin board to display it temporarily. Recycle to the box when the area is full.
- Set aside a shelf in your child's room or your family room for three-dimensional art projects. Eventually, you will decide whether they should be saved or tossed. Painted rocks can still look quite charming many years later.
- Involve your child in editing what gets tossed.
- As the years go by and you want to pare down the boxes, designate an area in a file cabinet that has your children's creations. This is how to be sure to save just a bit of it.
- Ask your mother what happened to all of your school papers.

ISN'T THAT MODERN ART?

You're not there to see them do the art, but you want the children to feel valued and loved when they bring the papers to you, so what do you keep? Are you insulting your children by tossing the papers?

When Ellen's son first went to preschool, he brought home truckloads of paintings every day. You know, they were the ones that looked as though they should be hanging at the Museum of Modern Art. She couldn't

---

throw them out. When she picked him up at a friend's house one day, she saw that they had papered a big wall in their kitchen with the art, which looked great. She found a good space in her house, and when she was overrun with the paintings, she learned to edit, usually out of his sight.

Get the Rest of Your House in Order: Prioritize

Go back to the beginning. Empty the house in your mind. Think about how you want to live. It's probably not with book bags here, coats there, toys and papers all over the place.

Ask yourself:

- Does my house have to be white-glove-inspection clean?
- Do I want to come home and relax or maintain the place?
- Do I need to be able to receive guests on a moment's notice?
- How often can I afford a housekeeper?
- Which rooms are most important to be clean?
- Am I ready to throw out my first apartment's stuff and my parents' hand-me-downs for real furniture?
- Do I need to hold onto my old college papers just in case?
- Do I want to do the garden and yard work myself?
- Can I do home repairs? And would I if I had the time?
- Do I want to paint and wallpaper?
- Can I maintain live plants and fresh flowers?
- Do I have time to do the laundry?
- Do I care that a room has a concept in which everything goes together?
- Do I resent cleaning?
- Are my children at an age that they can help?
- If my mother never had an interior designer, can I handle it without feeling frivolous?
- Can I make up my mind and live with it?

In case you're looking for priorities, here are four things to understand about your home:

- Enjoy it.
- Don't make your children afraid to go into a room.
- Respect your possessions.
- Buy the best you can afford; quality lasts longer.

MAKE THE LIVING ROOM A PLACE TO LIVE

When I was growing up, the living room was off-limits in most houses. One friend's living room had a rope barrier you usually see in bank lines at the door, and his mother would inspect the spotless white carpeting every night to make sure no one had set a sneakered foot on it.

Few of us live like that now. In fact, the living room, which seems to serve no purpose other than to receive the life insurance agent, is often turned into something else. Since the living room was the biggest area in Barbara's house, she turned it into an eat-in kitchen with a fireplace.

Deborah has turned her dining room into a music room. The family doesn't have to spend the time digging out instruments and music stands; they can be more spontaneous about playing together. They decided that they didn't really need a dining room and created a big space in their kitchen where they eat. They nixed formal dinner parties, too. Everybody's in the kitchen from family to honored guests.

Make Your Public Spaces As Efficient As Possible

When you come in after a long day at work, the last thing you want to look at is a ton of stuff piled up at the back door, then five billion little piles of detritus all over the house. It's depressing and gives you a horrible feeling of unease when you're at home.

- Reduce clutter.
- Think twice before you buy any more knickknacks.
- Throw out all those old magazines.
- Put hooks by the door for book bags and coats.
- Set an example: put your own coat away when you get home.
- Invest in an umbrella stand.
- Look at each room to see if there are pockets of space where you can put in shelves with doors. Some people call these cabinets. Perhaps you could rearrange the furniture to find these spaces.
- Keep one room decent so that you can immediately usher a guest in there. Even if it's the dining room, you can always sit around the table and have coffee.

TAKE TIME TO MAKE TIME

If you walk through your house and think about how you use it now and how it might work better for you, you'll probably decide that you need some work done. None of us lives with enough storage space.

You know that room near your kitchen that's always a mess—a dumping ground? It's the messy kitchen drawer that exploded. Build in bookshelves, have stacking boxes or baskets, and turn it into another sitting room, office, or computer room.

THINK ABOUT CALLING
A PROFESSIONAL TO HELP YOU

Kathy designs residential space. She helps with everything from floor plans to accessories, and her services are not as costly as you might imagine. Many working mothers who come to her are on a tight budget and have not used a designer before.

"They're afraid that I'll tell them they have to buy this, this, and this, that I have to travel to an exotic place to find everything. It's not so. Instead, a woman can ask for a one-hour consultation. I'll give her a contractor list of trusted people in the area, from plumbers to electricians, and she can use me as a reference to get the work done.

"People who come to me know generally what they want. My experience lets me describe the project more precisely to the contractor and obtain a more accurate bid. I know how many hours it should take to finish a job, and I can help women assess the estimates."

Her managing the project can save money since she knows how to recognize the quality of the job and can correct work before it turns into an expensive problem.

And she can save a mother time as well. One woman who was a pharmacist and the mother of two toddlers wanted to select wallpaper on her day off. "Taking them into a wallpaper store would be crazy," admits Kathy. "I brought books to her house, and we scheduled the meeting while her kids would be napping. Then I lined up an installer who would work half days, when her children were in preschool. With children you want a job finished as quickly as possible. Having materials around your house is dangerous, dirty, and dusty."

Fixer-upper, Reasonably Priced? Not for You

- Find a house that doesn't need work beyond carpeting, painting, wallpapering, and building some shelves. A new kitchen or bathroom or any demolition project is daunting.
- Don't begin to think about being your own contractor. Hire a professional contractor to negotiate prices, coordinate times for the work to be done, order and set the delivery dates for materials, and make sure that local inspections are made and permits are obtained.
- Make sure you hire reliable workers. Ask around. Never take a name from a list or a phone book without calling for references. Even when you get a reliable supplier, things don't always work out for the best.

Things are going to break. Here are the best ways to have work done when it never fits into your schedule:
- Ask for someone who will work on Saturdays. When they say no, use your power to cajole.
- Ask for the first appointment in the morning, and get to work an hour late.
- Have the job done the day your housekeeper comes.
- If it's a long job, such as painting or installing carpet or re-doing the basement walls, ask friends for references, for people you can trust to be alone in your house.
- Ask a friend or neighbor who works part-time to be at your house. Then reciprocate in kind.
- You don't need to be home for anybody who doesn't have to get into your house.

How to find people to get any job done:
- Start with friends and neighbors.
- Make sure your local plumber, carpenter, electrician, or heating contractor is familiar with your community and the way the houses are wired and how ducts and pipes are configured.

- Call your local city engineer for references. Since this department issues work permits and inspects jobs, they know who does the best work.
- Some plumbers or electricians who work for bigger firms will moonlight for you (at *your* convenience) on small jobs such as changing faucets or hanging light fixtures.
- Keep a list of people you use. When they're not available, ask them to recommend someone.

Thinking Ahead About Materials Can Save Time Later

CARPETING
- Select a twist or pattern, which will hide the dirt.
- Nylon wears well, but check to be sure it's treated with a stain-resistant chemical. Otherwise, know that Kool-Aid goes right into it.
- Wool absorbs stains.
- Rugs and carpeting absorb sound. That's important if you want to come home to a quieter environment.

KITCHEN FLOORS
- Get a no-wax floor. It's easiest.
- Ceramic tile is unforgiving. Everything that falls onto it breaks. . . and has to be cleaned up.
- Wood is great. A dark floor doesn't show dirt.

UPHOLSTERY
- Leather is best. It can last for thirty years if you take care of it.
- Make sure leather is dyed all the way through, not just colored on the surface. Kids can scratch off surface color.
- Clean leather with saddle soap or Windex.
- Cotton upholstery absorbs stains.

- Silk can be very strong, but wait until your children have gone to college.

WINDOW TREATMENTS
- Pleated shades can be cleaned easily.
- Vertical shades are noisy, and kids love to pull on them.
- Miniblinds are horrible dust collectors.
- If you use miniblinds choose plastic. Metal blinds will bend easily when kids grab them or throw balls at them. Once they're bent, that's it.

FURNITURE
- Choose wood over laminate. Laminate will scratch and cannot be repaired.
- Get a scratch-repair kit for your wood furniture, which can always be fixed.
- Condition your wood with lemon oil.

Give the Children a Playroom, a Place Mothers Never Go

Years ago, the idea of a playroom belonged only to the Prince of England. You know, playing in the nursery, eating nursery food, singing nursery rhymes. Now that we've become as busy with our careers as his mother, we've given over a room or a basement or an attic to the playroom.

If you're smart, you'll see it only every two weeks. Make it the last place to be picked up.
- Have little tables and chairs.
- Keep trains, dollhouses, car sets, little towns, kitchens, and the like set up there.
- Give them a television, and have plenty of shelves for the videos. (When they have a television in there, you don't have to hear the Saturday morning cartoons.)
- Make sure there's a door on that room.

- Forget about it, and let them destroy it with their friends. Let them jump on the old couch. Do the art projects in there. Drip paint and glue on the floor.
- Ban food from the playroom. You can't imagine what could be living in there two weeks from now.

THE METAMORPHOSIS OF THE PLAYROOM

- Toddlers and preschoolers: toy central, art room, block project room, cars and trucks room.
- School-age children: computer room, school project center, wild room with friends, the place for sleep-overs.
- Teenagers: place for very loud music, place to entertain friends without the connotation of a bedroom, place where they'd probably like to transform into their bedroom, to be—away from the rest of the family.

How to Have a Home Office

If you can work at home—for either all or part of your schedule—you must have a designated space.

You could start with a walk-in closet, then build in shelves and a desk. Capture a tiny portion of your basement or attic and make it a cozy spot to work. You won't take your business seriously if it's on the dining-room table. That's a hobby, not a business, and you'll find a million excuses not to work. Plus, you have to keep putting it all away so that the family can eat dinner.

The home office rules of order:
- Have enough space to hold all of your electronic equipment, and make sure it's sturdy furniture.
- Have a two- or four-drawer filing cabinet, and use it.

Remember, there was a support staff at the old office who used to do this for you. Now you have to make sure to keep track of clients and expenses.

- Put all your bills in one place.
- Tell your children, "If my phone is to my ear, you cannot talk to me."
- Tell your children, "Your desk is for coloring, not mine."

Learn to get rid of paper:
- You need a system, which is a tool and a habit.
- Your tool: TRAF (Toss, Refer, Action, File) for every piece of paper. Make it a habit.
- Do an initial sort with your mail—while standing. Some of it isn't worthy of hitting a desktop.
- Separate bills by which should be paid on the fifteenth or thirtieth of the month.
- If you want to get really good at this, hire a professional organizer. He or she will tell you how to sort piles into papers that are touched once, twice, and finished, how to make sense of the manila folders you have all over the place, and will give you a system for every office task you perform.

Needed: Light Housekeeping

Now we're treading into territory many working mothers have abandoned. For many it's difficult to do so because a sparkling clean house was the pride and joy of many of our mothers. Save your guilt for missing the first step and bonding with the fourth-grade teacher. What does it mean to be a mother who can't keep the house clean? Not so much.

CLEANING CAN TAKE ITS TOLL

Laurel says, "I used to come home from work and clean the whole house. It would make me mean. For my sanity, I had to lower my standards. Now I don't even see the kitchen floor. I know it's dirty, but I can't notice it. My sheets are changed when I have a minute."

Elizabeth concurs: "My house doesn't look the way I'd like it to. It took me a while to let go of all the responsibilities. I have my kids help clean, and when my daughter forgets some of the dusting, I have to remember that it's okay."

Release the Cleaning to Someone Else

There are many options available.

- Cleaning services consist of automatons who come in to your house and clean furiously for a prescribed number of hours. The services are listed in the Yellow Pages.
- Hire a housekeeper to come daily, weekly, or semi-monthly.
- Combine the services. Use a cleaning service a few times a year for the heavy-duty work, and have a regularly scheduled housekeeper for maintenance.

How to choose a housekeeper:

- Ask friends, relatives, and colleagues for references, or check the classified ads.
- Recognize that if you have high standards of cleanliness no one will meet them.
- Before you meet her, walk through your house and make a list of everything you would like done weekly (remember vacuuming under the bed and getting all the cobwebs).
- Make a wish list of things you'd do if this were your day job or what you'd want an ideal housekeeper to do. This

can include dreadful jobs such as taking all the cushions off the sofa and vacuuming it, moving the furniture to find all the crayons under it, or washing windows.

- Then meet her in person, and walk her through your house.
- Tell her how you like things done, which towels go in which bathroom, which sheets on which bed, and how the wood floors and your grandmother's table should be cleaned.
- Don't feel guilty about asking for what you want—remember you're paying for it. Don't worry—if she doesn't want to do it, she won't—or she'll quit.
- Minimize the confrontations you will have, especially if she's going to be spending any part of the day with your child.
- Ask for references, and be sure to call them. Ask whether she did extra tasks willingly and whether they trusted her with a key and the alarm code.
- Hire her on a trial basis for a couple of weeks.
- Tell her the salary, or ask her hourly rate. Know what your friends are paying before you enter into this negotiation.
- Communicate by notes. Leave lists of what you want done. Have her leave lists of more cleaning supplies you need to buy.
- If she's honest, shows up at the appointed time, cleans fairly decently, and lessens your aggravation, forget it when she doesn't wipe the top of the refrigerator even though you asked her to. Do it yourself or realize that nobody's going to notice anyway.
- Understand at the outset that she can quit at any time.

MAKE SURE YOU
COMMUNICATE EARLY WHAT YOU WANT

Rebecca is a busy attorney and didn't want to come home to buckets and mops. "I wanted her day completed when I got home," she says. "I didn't want to walk in and hear the washer going."

The first time I actually prepared the chore list and the wish list, I took a prospective cleaning woman through the house and pointed everything out. "Oh, I know what you want," she smiled, "a tie-your-hair-on-top-of-your-head old-fashioned cleaner the way our mothers used to do it."

"Right," I smiled and nodded.

"Well, you can forget about that," she told me. "Who has the energy?" Indeed. That was my point.

Gene got some unexpected bonuses. "I've had my housekeeper for seventeen years, and I'm completely intimidated by her," says Gene. "I'm never home and always in a rush, so I'm sure she thinks I have a screw loose. She even arranges my furniture without asking. It's usually better. When I finally decided to get grown-up draperies, I had a decorator come in to show me how they would hang. My housekeeper said, 'Show them to her closer to the floor. They'll be much better.'

"Once when I had her stay overnight with the children, I'd made dinner, and my daughter turned up her nose at it. My housekeeper turned to her and said, 'Eat your dinner. Your mother made it. She's doing the best she can.'"

You Want to Clean It Yourself?

If your standards cannot be compromised, you have to find the time to do it.

Try not to take it all on yourself. Discover very early whether you have a partner who is willing to help clean up. Just be sure it can get done if he's not going to help.

Recruit your built-in workforce—your children. If you have a son who's vacuuming, wiping the kitchen counters, and throwing his own dirty gym clothes in the washer, think what a wonderful adult male you are grooming.

- Money talks. Give a kid a nickel a day to make a bed.
- Buy them something they want, and keep it contingent upon making their beds.
- Have your child clean with you. Along the way, give little tips so they know they're doing the job correctly.
- Assign tasks you're not particularly crazy about. You never know; your child just might like it.
- Encourage any cleaning chore they like, from cleaning mirrors to mopping the kitchen floor. Don't criticize too much. Just be helpful. And don't do it over again yourself.

Get a Handle on the Cleaning

If you manage a bit during the week, then your cleaning chores on the weekend are lessened. Nobody wants to spend a weekend cleaning the house. We have determined that housekeeping is not a measure of our self-worth.

What to clean or tidy every morning to have an illusion of cleanliness when you come home:
- Have comforters on the beds that you can pull up quickly.
- Put the dishes in the dishwasher and wipe the counters after breakfast.
- Pick up the clutter.
- Get rid of yesterday's newspapers.
- In the bathrooms, pick up the towels and put things away in cabinets.

How to clean on Saturday morning:

- Wear a Walkman.
- Or send everybody out of the house, and put music on very loud.
- Determine beforehand what really needs to be cleaned.
- Make sure you have enough supplies and a carrier, plus a bucket.
- Vacuuming does wonders for the cleaning illusion, especially on wood floors.
- Clean kitchen and bathrooms thoroughly once a week.
- Don't forget the kitchen and bathroom floors.
- If you don't use a room much, don't spend too much time cleaning it. Concentrate on heavy-use areas.
- Every once in a while, do the bucket and rag thing on the baseboards.
- Give yourself a time limit.

THE KARMA OF CLEANING

There is something funny about cleaning. Once you get beyond the emotion, it becomes hypnotic. Not only that, you really accomplish something. I like to finish a room, then walk out and reenter to see how different it looks. You don't always get that satisfaction at work. Your projects might be more difficult to quantify and evaluate. It's a cinch to know if you got the cleaning right.

Though Deborah is financially secure today, it wasn't always so. She was raised in New York City's East Harlem neighborhood, where cleaning truly was a way for a mother to feel worthy. So it keeps a special meaning for Deborah. "Order and cleanliness are important to me," she says, "and I like to clean. One night I stood at the kitchen sink scrubbing all the pot bottoms as my mother used to do. It gave me a connection to all the women who had come before me. I thought, 'We have all been in this place.'"

But Do You Want to Do the Laundry?

My sister-in-law went back to work a few years ago, and I wondered how she was going to get all her laundry done. In our family she's Queen of the Laundry. It seemed like a load was always in the washer or dryer and that another was about to go downstairs. I asked her how she does it now, and she told me her secret: "I never leave the house without putting in a load."

- Give over the laundry to the housekeeper you have hired.
- Relax if it's not folded just so.
- Send it out to a local Laundromat, drop it off on your way to work, and pick it up on your way home.
- Ironing? Are you kidding? Your dryer is your iron. Fold the stuff as soon as it comes out of the dryer, and it will look just fine.
- Send your husband's shirts out.

What to Do with Clothes Your Children Outgrow

This monster threatens to devour any storage space sitting silently unaware in your home. The best tip is to keep on top of it. You may prefer to donate, or have a tag, garage, or yard sale.

- Keep an extra laundry basket marked "donate" next to your washer so that you have a place to put old clothes when the urge hits you.
- Be merciless in getting rid of your kids' toys and clothes.
- Donate at least twice a year.
- If you haven't worn something in two years, get rid of it. Don't think twice. Don't miss it.
- Find cousins, a charity, a church, a homeless shelter, or an abused women's group you can give to regularly.
- Find a charity that will pick up. Some will call you every month—it's a great impetus to weed out your closets.

- If you're going to have a sale, put a price on something the minute you put it into the "tag sale" box.

How to Have a Great Sale

- Set a date at least a month in advance. It takes longer than you think to coordinate this.
- Advertise in your local paper. Ask if they can give you signs and balloons to mark the way to your house. Use them.
- Be ready early. Even though you say "No early birds" in your ad, they'll show up at 6:30 A.M.
- Have as much merchandise as possible. The more cluttered, the better.
- If you don't have enough for a big sale, consolidate the block and have everybody contribute. It's less exhausting to work at a sale with more helpers, too.
- Put out tables to display small stuff.
- Have prices on everything or fill boxes with everything at the same price.
- Haggle. Your customers expect it.
- To get your children to part with their possessions, tell them that they can have the proceeds from their own stuff.
- Have your kids run the lemonade and cookie stand, and let them keep the profits.
- Anything unsold gets donated, preferably the next day. Call charities to find out which will pick up at your home.

A Year of Living Neatly

January: Make a resolution to get organized. Carry it out: make a list of what needs to be pared down and figure out how it's going to be done.

February: Toss accumulated magazines. Face the piles in the attic and basement.

March: Check to make sure you have enough storage space. If you need more space, call contractors to do work before their busy season. Clean *your* closet and drawers.

April: Toss accumulated magazines. Check the kids' spring clothes to see what you need to buy.

May: Start seriously collecting clothes and extra stuff for donations or sale.

June: Toss accumulated magazines. Final edit of the school year's memory box.

July: Tag sale/Donate

August: Toss accumulated magazines. Make room in drawers for new school clothes.

September: Get the big box ready for school papers.

October: Toss accumulated magazines. Put away summer clothes. Decide what to donate. Bring the summer furniture inside. (It will get ruined by the winter, honest.)

November: Have donated clothes picked up. Gradually begin maintenance projects (i.e., silver polishing, furniture repair) for the holidays.

December: Toss accumulated catalogs.

So is it worth it? Should you clean up the house, make sure there are fresh towels and plenty of shelving? It seems like it. Just don't let it get out of proportion. Don't make cleanliness the ultimate goal. It's a means to an end. An uncluttered environment gives you more space to enjoy your family.

▦ 3 ▦

Providing Food for Starving Children—Yours

What is "something to eat"?

I can open a cupboard in my kitchen at any time and pretty quickly put together a meal that's tasty and gives a nod to the food pyramid, too. Yet most of my family members could open the same cupboard and see only a barren wasteland.

Perhaps these meals are revealed only to me, and the inspiration evades them all completely. That, and the fact that they often have to find their own forms of breakfast, lunch, dinner, and snacks when I'm not around to concoct it for them makes me attempt to fill up the kitchen with foods that are easily constructed into "something to eat" in the family's requisite two minutes or less.

Mothers also have a nagging pull to eat meals together à la Family Cleaver, as well as a fear that a kid's annual checkup will reveal that nothing green and leafy has passed the lips for the past year. We have a heightened awareness of eating disorders and pudgy couch potatoes and rampant tooth decay, plus a picky eater or two to deal with.

So . . . let's eat.

Sitting Down Together

For most of us, dinner is the meal on which to concentrate. Yes, you have to have the usual cereal, frozen waffles, juice, milk, and bread around for breakfast, but that's easy. Of course you stock up on sliced meats (How did we live before wiggly processed turkey took over our lives?), fruit, cookies, and the ubiquitous juice boxes for lunch (and we'll get to the subcategory of snacks), but dinner is the meal tied into family life.

That's when we realize the image of conversations, togetherness, and communication. But it's a huge deal to get the family home, settled, and properly fed in the evening. If you have made dinner together your goal, and if you ever accomplish it, pat yourself on the back.

WHEN YOU CAN'T MAKE DINNER

Many working mothers can't get the family together for a proper dinner, and as your children get older and more involved with activities, and more peculiar in their eating habits ("I'll just have a baked potato, please" or "Tofu and brown rice for me" or "I only have time for a bagel"), you may turn, as many have, to sharing breakfast. In her role as a CEO, Shelly goes to many business dinners during the week, so she and her husband always have breakfast together. The kids aren't always there, but the parents have time to connect.

Single mother Andrea also has evening commitments. "I make the morning meal our big meal," she says. "I've even lit candles. I set it up the night before, and my son and I get up earlier to have this

---

time together. We're both energetic and fresh, and get to anticipate our days. We have a good dinner once or twice a week. Other times, the microwave is the cook, and I eat standing up."

What Do You Eat?

However you dine, you still have to bring the food into the house and prepare it. You might be making a nice living, but you're certainly not going out to dinner or dining on take-out every single night.

Like everything else, this calls for a system. Figuring out in advance what to eat, how to make it, and how to get it to the table will save you time in the supermarket and anxiety on your way home from work.

How to Decide What You're Going to Eat

- Know something about nutrition.
- Specialize in a few dishes, and save your experimentation and mission to expand your family's food tastes for the weekends.
- Seek out easy recipes from relatives, friends, magazines, newspapers, television cooking shows, and cookbooks.
- For school potluck suppers, have people bring recipes. They usually make dishes their children eat.
- Keep a file of your family's favorite recipes.
- Plan for a month of meals, if possible.
- Stick to your meal plan, and post it on the refrigerator.
- Invest in a Crock-Pot, and learn to use it. This appliance seems to be making a big comeback. You load it up in the morning, then you or your sitter turn it off right before dinner.
- Learn to cook those one-dish casseroles you can make ahead and freeze.

Here's What Families Are Eating
(Based on an Entirely Unscientific Study)

- Lots of pasta—from spaghetti with tomato sauce to stuffed shells to simple sautéed veggie sauces
- Tacos and burritos and fajitas
- Meat loaf (often with ground turkey)
- Chili
- Steak
- Pork chops
- Roasts (beef, pork, chicken, turkey) made in advance, reheated, and then recycled during the week with quick sauces or pasta
- Chicken breasts sautéed in a grill pan
- Hearty bean and vegetable soups, bread, salad
- Ham
- Lasagna
- Frozen or canned vegetables
- Stir-fry
- Make-your-own pizza with veggies and leftover meats
- Make-your-own sandwiches with lots of ingredients

TIP FOR BABIES

If you gag when you open a jar of baby food, and feel horribly guilty about resorting to its convenience, you can spend just an hour on a weekend making food for a week and freezing it in individual portions. It's quite easy. Smells good, too.

- Meats: Poach skinless chicken, cubes of trimmed beef, or lamb in water until thoroughly cooked. Purée in a food processor or grind in a blender, adding some of the cooking water as you need it to make a fine paste. Freeze in ice cube trays. Pop out portions as you need them. As your baby grows, you use more cubes, of course.

> - Vegetables: Boil any vegetables in a small amount of water until thoroughly cooked. Then follow the directions for meats.

Visiting the Supermarket: A Respite from the World

Go at the right time, and it can actually be relaxing and mesmerizing. Fortunately, markets are open twenty-four hours these days, or at least until 11 P.M. Even though you might be a person who needs to get to bed early, it saves you tons of time to go late—or at the crack of dawn before work.

There are plenty of carts available, short lines at the checkout counter, and no pileups in the aisles. You have time to peruse the labels and find out whether you are providing a modicum of nutrition to your family. When you go alone, it's much faster because you don't have to debate with your children every item that goes into the cart.

OLDER KIDS CAN COOK

Children twelve and older can plan and prepare dinners. It gives them family responsibility, the ability to identify with you, and cooking skills. It gives you tremendous help.

Assign a child this job each week. Sit down together on Saturday to go through cookbooks and plan the menus. Set any rules (i.e., must include a vegetable, can't have the same thing every night). Shop and do as much advance work as possible on the weekend.

The reward: the child who cooks doesn't have to set the table or do the dishes.

AN ARGUMENT AGAINST THAT CATCH-A-FEW-MINUTES KIND OF SHOPPING

Heather, who's an executive assistant, rushed from her office one afternoon to drive her high-school daughter to her soccer game. Since Heather had seen her daughter play many times before, she didn't feel so terrible running over to the nearby supermarket to pick up ingredients for dinner. She waved good-bye to her daughter, told her to wait at the field, and she'd be back to pick her up.

"After forty-five minutes of shopping," recalls Heather, "I went through the checkout line, and when I looked up at the windows, I saw that it was pouring rain, complete with lightning and thunder that I hadn't even heard when I was shopping. Criticizing myself as a horrible mother who didn't even know it had started raining, I jumped in the car and drove very fast to the field, expecting that my daughter had probably gone home with a friend. No, she was standing there, soaked from the downpour. When I questioned her she said, 'But you told me not to leave!' Ah, guilt."

How to Shop Efficiently

- Take a list if you know you always forget something.
- Or don't take a list if you know enough about cooking to be inspired by the ingredients.
- Do big shopping once a week. Try not to go during the week unless you run out of something.
- If your housekeeper or sitter shops for you, make a list of items that should always be in the house that are her responsibility to get.
- Shop at a big cost-cutting warehouse once a month to stock up on paper products and nonperishables.
- Give yourself a time limit. Things can really get out of hand in there.

- Buy enough to be able to make extra food in case a child's friend stays for dinner.
- Condition your family to love one easy dish, and keep the staples so you can always whip it up. (Pasta comes to mind.)
- Consult with your family before shopping to find out if tastes in cereals, juices, and snacks have changed in the last week. Anything is possible.

TAKE TIME TO MAKE TIME

Put a complete shopping list on your computer, listing the specific brands you like. That way, when you print out the list and check off the items you need, anybody from your husband to your sitter to your mother can do the shopping and get exactly what you want.

HAVE A FAMILY MEMBER OR BABY-SITTER
DO THE PREP WORK BEFORE YOU COME HOME

"I have the sitter cut up ingredients for a stir-fry," says Moira. "I ask her to peel potatoes and put them in a pot of cold water and boil them, but I mash them myself. It's easier to have somebody do that than to explain how you like your potatoes mashed."

Who's Cooking?

Cooking can be a lot of fun, but that's mostly on the weekends when you have time to do it. Cutting, chopping, dragging out the pans, sautéing, boiling, and broiling are not pleasures during the week.

Besides, you have to change your clothes so you don't get the suit messed up—but if you're late getting home, then you don't have time to change, and if you're eating fast to run to parents' night at school, then you barely have time to eat anyway.

How to make dinner without going crazy:

- Spend a few hours on Sunday preparing as much as you can freeze so that someone (husband, baby-sitter, child) can get a meal started before you walk in the door.
- Make one meal per evening. When my son was a newborn, my pediatrician warned me to never get in the habit of making a different meal for everybody.
- Don't get bent out of shape when your kid won't eat the dinner. You don't have that much emotion invested in it in the first place. Point to the options: the boxes of cereal.
- Try to arrange it so that only one part of the meal has to be prepared when you get home. Have either the entree or vegetables made in advance. You are not an executive chef with assistants who are all around you cooking the dishes; getting everything to the table together is hard to do alone.
- Buy vegetables that are already cut up.
- If you stop at a salad bar for lunch, make a big salad at the same time for your family dinner.
- Have a creative plan for the leftovers so that they are not completely recognizable as boring and revolting.
- As long as you're cooking, make extras. Prepare two lasagnas on Sunday, for example, or bake more potatoes than you need for a meal, and do something with them the next day.
- Be as specific as possible, or as you need to be, with a husband who is getting dinner ready. Sometimes he needs to know exactly what to make or the ingredients set out for him that morning.
- Let your kids help with setting the table when they're little and with preparing the meal as they get older.

HOW TO EAT WELL AND AVOID COOKING, EVER

When Karen was raising her two children, she worked full-time as a secretary in a real-estate office. She loved to cook and would come home every night and put something together, without advance planning.

Today she runs a business shopping and cooking for working mothers who break out in a sweat just thinking about those chores. She plans two weeks of meals, shops, cooks in her clients' homes, and stocks the freezer. She leaves complete instructions on how to reheat a dish, promising that dinner will be on the table within thirty minutes.

Many mothers ask her to help them do what they don't have time to do: change their diets to cut down on fats or calories, red meat or processed foods, or to include more vegetables and beans. And here are some of the most popular dishes:

- Hearty soups
- Stews such as beef Bourguignonne (which is making a comeback)
- Meat loaf
- Meatballs
- Rice pilaf
- Twice-baked potatoes
- Mashed potatoes
- Lasagna
- Fish (wrap it well in plastic and paper, and yes, it will freeze just fine)
- Rice and beans
- Roast chicken (free-range chickens are popular)
- Chicken with orange sauce (no one asks for heavy sauces or gravies)
- Stuffed pastas

Karen's toughest customers are picky eaters. If you have one, she suggests you take your child to the frozen-food section of the supermarket and look at the enticing photographs of the prepared dishes. Your child has a much better idea than if you just say the words "Salisbury steak."

To find this kind of business in your community, check your local parenting paper or phone your chamber of commerce. Though it's not inexpensive, the cost is not prohibitive. You could even choose to use a service just during your busy season at work.

Anyone for a Snack?

Here's one time you don't have to encourage your children to eat. Did you ever notice how they're starving to death (death!) between meals? This is also when you have a nutrition nightmare. With young children, you're in complete snack control and can make sure that all they're getting is an extra handful or two of Cheerios, or a few more apple slices.

When they get older and need that after-school burst, you're not around to see what they're choosing—but if you provide the snacks, then they can only eat what's around. As far as chips and candy bars after school goes, you can't stop your kids from buying them. You can just send them out with the right information, then hope they use it.

TIP FOR TEENAGERS

Judy controls the somewhat junky snacks her children eat by supplying them at home and making them pay for them. "My teenagers have after-school jobs, so every payday each of us puts ten dollars in a jar. That's our snack money. They don't like to spend their own money on total junk, so they'll go to the bulk discounter and buy four-pound cans of pretzels and lots of microwave popcorn."

Involve Your Children in Their Snacks

This way, they eat only the good snacks you have them prepare and don't eat the bushels of greasy, salty little crackers
and gooey sweets. Not all the time, anyway. Here are some
no-recipe, make-it-yourself favorites:

- Quesadillas—Lay flour tortillas open on a baking sheet.
  Put a thin layer of salsa or spaghetti sauce on the tortilla.
  Cover half the tortilla with shredded cheese of your
  choice (Monterey Jack, cheddar, or mozzarella). Fold the
  other half over. Bake in a preheated 350° oven for five
  minutes. Cut each into three triangles.
- Ants on a Log—Spread a long pretzel stick with peanut
  butter. Stick raisins (these are the ants) into the peanut
  butter.
- Better Than Apple Slices—Core an apple and cut it into
  slices. Spread each slice with a layer of peanut butter and
  a thin layer of honey. Dot with raisins or sunflower seeds
  or both.
- Fruit Kabobs—Cut up a whole bunch of favorite fruits
  into chunks. You can do this the night before to make
  the snack faster. Put on sticks, and enjoy. You can also
  prepare a yogurt or strawberry jam dip for these.

I thought that food and cooking was an area that made
most working mothers nuts. Then I found Ruth, a human
resources executive.

"I love food shopping," she says. "I love to cook, and I
love to eat. I can't wait to plan all the meals, and then make
sure I have the right ingredients. I spend lots of time cooking on the weekends, and I make extra food to have during
the week."

Isn't it nice that she wants to be so involved?

"Well," she says, "I'd trade it all for being attuned to
what's going on at school."

So you see we all have our areas of expertise, even at
home.

▦ 4 ▦

Confronting
Your Fears:
Choosing Child Care

Welcome to the top of the guilt list. You could spend months and years here, feeling terrible about leaving a tiny, adorable infant who has yet to sit up, much less take a step or say "Mama." You could make yourself miserable fretting that your toddler spends the day watching far too much Barney.

A better tactic is to dry your tears, try to suck it up, and center your concentration on finding quality child care for them.

Go into the search with your eyes wide open. To do that, you're going to need a lot of information: about selecting from the options for different ages, finding and hiring people and services, checking up on them, leaving your children home alone, arranging playdates, and coping with emergencies such as snow days and sick days.

No matter what arrangement you select, make sure to check credentials and references.

WHY I LIKE GOING TO WORK

"If I stayed home, I couldn't do snack at ten o'clock, letters at eleven, lunch at noon, numbers at one, playground at two while I also clean the house and do the laundry and make dinner. I'm better with my children when I come home from work."

—Cyndi, a bank marketing director

What Are You Looking For?

Start out with the right assumption. You don't want a substitute for yourself, you cannot possibly find someone who loves your children as much as you do, and you don't want to hire someone who secretly (or sometimes not so secretly) wants to be you.

Your needs will change as the years go on.

- For a tiny baby, you will feel a lot better having a person with a great deal of experience. You might be a neophyte in the baby business yourself, especially if you didn't have younger siblings, didn't baby-sit much, or don't have older nieces and nephews living close by.
- If you're thinking of in-home care, look for an older woman. Some cities have consortiums of older women who care for babies, such as one in Philadelphia called Dial-a-Granny. Ask at local churches and senior centers for services like this one in your community.
- Older children are going to need somebody who has the energy and flexibility to get down on the floor or romp or do finger painting.
- A younger, experienced person, either in your home or at a child-care center, is likely to work out better. By

then, you'll be more confident, too, in your own abilities as a mother.

How to Determine Which Kind of Child Care Is Right for You

- Look for child care that works for you at the moment. Your situation is tenuous, temporary, ever-changing. Heaven knows how your needs will change in a year.
- Think about your schedule: your hours, your flexibility, your unplanned meetings, your travel, your early morning commitments.
- Assess what you need from cooking to cleaning to laundry to shopping to driving.
- Keep in mind your children's schedules: classes, playdates, birthday parties.

MARY POPPINS? NOT QUITE

Our family's child-care history looks like a modern résumé, hardly the straight and narrow climb up the corporate ladder from mailroom to line management at the same Fortune 500 firm. We've had a slew of baby-sitters, from the lovely grandmother types to students to nurses to women who sat glued to the television all day long, to a live-in nanny who lasted for a whopping two weeks, and five day-care centers. This is typical. Don't worry if it happens to you.

Don't Expect Child Care to Be Everything

- No child care is perfect. You make trade-offs, and you must schedule the time to supply what's missing. If you want more story time, for instance, read to your child at night or get up earlier in the morning.

- When your children develop an intense loving bond to their caregivers, try not to let your feelings of alarm, intimidation, jealousy, and abandonment—not to mention inadequacy—overrun your entire life. Recognize that you have these natural emotions, then understand that your child and caregiver can't help it when they're spending huge blocks of time together. Gulp and be thankful.

Both your children and caregiver know that you are Mommy, the one who establishes the values, lays down the law, and gives the most kisses. No matter how many hours you're away, you're still going to be the most important woman to your children.

Understand the Options, and Weigh the Pros and Cons—but Hurry, You'll Be Late for Work

DAY CARE
Pro
- You can drop your child off very early.
- If you choose the right place with a good facility that includes such bonuses as thinking toys and computers and some kind of educational enrichment, along with a quality staff, your child can stay in the center until kindergarten.
- Socializing starts early.
- Breakfast or lunch may be included.
- They can have great large motor toys and lots of blocks.
- They organize field trips.
- They're reliable every day.

Con
- There can be high turnover of staff and children.
- Less attention may be paid to your child than what you'd prefer.

- Staff may not be great with individualized development (bottle-to-cup weaning, toilet training).
- Children get sick more often.
- You have to make other plans if your child is sick.
- There's no flexibility on pick-up times.
- All the dreadful chores at home are up to you. Nobody's coming in every day to help.

FITTING DAY CARE TO YOUR NEEDS

Cyndi: "I wanted a place very close to home that would take the children three days a week because my mother watches them the other two days. I found a place I liked, but they didn't have part-time for children under two, so I was paying to have both of them in for all five days. I liked the center, and I would bring them big mugs of pens from the bank where I work, bring cookies at Christmas, and give them everything they could use I hadn't sold at garage sales. I was just looking for goody points because I can't do the kind of volunteer activities they ask for during the day. But after a while the director said to me, 'Why don't you just pay for the days your boys are here?' We have a mutual loyalty."

Jean: "I didn't want a large open space because I was concerned about germs, so I looked for a place that had separate rooms for each age level. I didn't want the bigger children playing with the crawling children in the ride-on toy room either. I also wanted to come by at lunchtime and nurse my baby, so I found a center that would not push formula."

Kelley: "We don't live in a Beaver Cleaver neighborhood with kids running in and out of houses all day, so when my children were each about two, I gave up the in-home baby-sitter and opted for day care. It helped with socialization."

Lynn: "I was concerned about communication and knowing what my son was doing there. I found a center that had each caregiver write a little note every day that told you what the children ate, how they felt, and then a sentence or two that was personal. My son is twelve, and I've saved them all."

Betty: "When our first child was born, I hired a colleague who had left the company to be a stay-at-home mother to come in and watch my baby. But she wasn't giving the time to help the baby develop. She was just taking my child on her errands every day. Finally, we put him into day care and saw a tremendous change. He was suddenly eager to learn."

IN-HOME DAY CARE

Pro

- In this situation, in which a woman takes children into her home—often to be part of a group with her own preschooler—your child will probably get more individualized attention.
- The environment is more like home.
- The group is smaller.
- It's not terribly expensive.

Con

- It won't have as many toys, books, and play equipment as a day-care center.
- The caregiver can be overwhelmed by the demands of caring for so many children of varying ages by herself.
- Home may not be spacious enough for all the children.

WHEN HOME DAY CARE WORKS

Delia: "We moved to a new community, and I didn't know much about the child care there, and I didn't have time to do a lot of research before I had to start my job. I met a woman at the playground who took care of four children in her home. It seemed right to

> us, and our toddler made friends quickly. Also, if I were
> fifteen minutes late picking up my daughter, it wasn't
> so terrible because this woman was already home."

AU PAIR

Pro

- This international program that sends young English-speaking women from European countries to live in your home for one-year stints is best for mothers who work at home and need a mother's helper.
- They can be like family members.
- This option is the least expensive live-in care.
- Agencies give you several candidates to choose from.
- You can interview your candidate before she comes to live with you.
- The agency provides her health care as well as a support network.

Con

- They work only a forty-five-hour week.
- You pay their plane fare plus room and board.
- They are young and inexperienced.
- You can feel as though you have another child whose emotional needs must be attended to.
- They are not permitted to stay alone overnight with your children.
- The turnover and limited hours could be difficult.

THE BEST RELATIONSHIP WITH AN AU PAIR

Eleanor: "We've had several au pairs, and our children like them. I do very specific schedules at the beginning of the year so she knows exactly what to do, from packing lunch, going through the school backpacks to make sure we get all the notes, to arranging playdates. I don't really know the other mothers; she does."

NANNY

Pro

- This live-in caregiver—not a baby-sitter or au pair—is an experienced woman who may or may not have formal training.
- Give her a comfortable spot in your home for her to live, preferably with her own bathroom or one she shares with only the children.
- You have the freedom to get to the office at 7:30 A.M. and stay late.
- You can return home to find lots of chores done.
- This kind of care is the ultimate convenience.
- She knows and loves your child.
- A baby can be on his or her own schedule.
- She can become very close to your family.
- If she drives, she can do car pools.

Con

- You have to be able to deal with having someone in your space.
- It's expensive.
- You have to be careful not to take advantage of her.
- It may be rather difficult to fire a woman who has moved in to your home.

LIVING WITH THE CHOICE OF A NANNY

Amy: "My schedule varies so widely that it was making me crazy to find people to come in at different times and on different days. Everyone wanted a regular schedule. Also, my children are not that close in age, so I needed someone who could stay with the little one at home and pick up the older one at school. Sometimes I asked her to work on weekends, too. I feel guilty about all of this, but we have taken her on vacation with us and given her plenty of time to herself."

Maggie: "I made it very clear that I wanted my own sense of space and that I didn't want her being a part of our family on weekends."

Alice: "Our nanny came from a different part of the country and would tell us about her family who wanted to come to visit. One was her brother, whom she described as 'on parole' after his brush with the law for being 'wrongly convicted' of dropping his child. That was enough for us. It was as if she were telling us to fire her. So we did. Naturally, none of this had come up in the interview."

BABY-SITTER

Pro

- She comes in every morning when you ask her to (hopefully).
- She can do some of your errands, cleaning, cooking, and laundry. You define the job based on your needs.
- The benefits of live-in help if you don't have the space or the inclination.
- She can probably be flexible enough to stay late or help out on weekends.

Con

- When she's sick or late, you have to find coverage.
- Don't expect great child-development skills.

THE STAND FOR SITTERS

Betty: "I interviewed twenty women for the baby-sitting job. I prayed every night to find one; I never prayed more in my life. I finally found one. I am blessed, and I have such peace of mind. She raised five boys of her own, she bakes with my kids, drives them, and starts our dinner. I put the laundry in every morning, and she moves it to the dryer, then folds the children's clothes and puts them away. I don't expect her to clean the house, just to straighten the family room where the children play."

Carol: "We had a full-time sitter when my son was little. She was wonderful. I told her when I hired her that I had one requirement: she could *not* be late because I had a very unforgiving boss."

Ricki: "I want to be able to take my daughter to nursery school twice a week, so I ask the sitter to come in late those days and just pick her up and bring her home. It's nice for me and for the sitter because I often ask her to stay late."

RELATIVES

Pro

- This arrangement can be heaven for a grandparent who wants to have a close relationship with your children.
- Great for you because you know your relatives love your children.
- This kind of relationship works best for a limited time (not birth to kindergarten, five days a week) in conjunction with another kind of child care.
- You must insist on compensating them in a regular way. If not cash, then vacations or stock or something else valuable and tangible.

Con

- Emotionally expensive. Your mother has already raised children and is probably looking forward to a life like a regular grandparent: enjoy them for a while, then go back home and deal with other adults.
- You are employing your relatives.
- Be sure not to abuse the kindness of relatives.

DEALING WITH RELATIVES A WHOLE NEW WAY

Bonnie: "Monday through Thursday my father-in-law picks up my daughter at nursery school and has her for the afternoon. It's a nice relationship for them, and he really looks forward to it."

Jane: "My mother-in-law takes the children every day and spoils them like crazy, buying every single thing they ask for. I find it impossible to say anything to her, and my husband doesn't seem to mind, but I feel it undermines everything I try to teach."

There's More Than One Way to Find a Baby-sitter

The sitters who begin when your child comes home from the hospital and leave when your child packs up for college are not the norm. You'll probably run through them like a river, but that's the nature of the business. You're going to get very good at finding a new sitter very quickly.

- **Ask everybody you know.** Get the word out at work, at the gym, in your reading group, at your church or synagogue, on your block. This is the penultimate networking experience. Cash in all your chips.
- **Ask other baby-sitters.** Go to a local playground one day during your lunch hour when the baby-sitters are out there with the kids. Ask if they have friends or if they're about to leave a job if, say, the child they care for will be going to kindergarten.
- **Call any local colleges.** Many times students, especially graduate students, have schedules that give them plenty of time they can give to you. And there's no doubt they need the money.
- **Call a hospital with a nursing school.** These women can be wonderful, especially with tiny babies.
- **Place a classified ad.** Make it very specific, and put it in a local community paper. That way you know it will be

easier for someone to find your house, know your area, and be able to get to you when it snows two feet overnight.

It's very time-consuming and difficult to assess the candidates who call you. You can receive an overwhelming number of calls. At some point, you may become desperate enough to spend the money for an agency.

- **Call an agency.** They'll work with you to find the person who can fulfill your needs, but bear in mind that they're often working from classified ads, so you can end up hearing from the same people. A great advantage is that the sitters are licensed and bonded (should be, anyway), and the agency will give you a trial period to make sure things work out. An agency is expensive, but they guarantee to find you someone for the fee.

Of course, everyone can tell you a horror story, so be sure to check the agency with the Better Business Bureau to make sure complaints have not been filed against them. Even agencies will send candidates who are not properly qualified.

Now You Have to Conduct the Interview

Serious candidates for in-home child care or out-of-home centers should be interviewed more than once. *Always* take the time to check references. Assume nothing. And remember that nothing is permanent. You could be doing this again very soon.

What you should ask at a day-care center:
- To see the entire facility, including outside play spaces, and where children eat and nap.
- To see where diapers are changed and how they are disposed of.
- To see the toys/learning materials.

- What is the curriculum?
- What is the experience of the caregivers?

What you should know about a prospective nanny or sitter:
- Personal history, including her age, where she grew up, and why she wants to be your sitter
- Employment history
- Three references
- Driving record
- What she would you do if . . . Everything from your child's being sick to her being unable to come in for the day to an emergency in your home
- Her views on disciplining children
- How she typically spends a day with a child the age of yours
- Whether she has CPR training
- Why she left her last job
- Whether she can be flexible about working late, traveling with your family, or working on weekends
- Her salary requirements

TAKE TIME TO MAKE TIME

You could be kicking yourself if you don't check the references. Listen carefully when you do. Trust your instincts. If another mother is not gushing over the sitter or seems to hold back a bit, take it as a warning siren. Here's what you want to know:
- Is this really a former employer, and not a friend or relative?
- What kinds of duties she had
- Why she left
- How she handled an emergency
- How she got along with the children
- A description of her personality, appearance, and demeanor

Background checks are gaining in popularity. There are several agencies, both local and national, that can help you. Look for an ad in your local parenting paper or in the Yellow Pages under "security."

You want a security check that gives you information on a criminal record (usually done by county), driving records, and financial records, including check bouncing.

Negotiating the Salary

Find out what families in your community are paying. Then start with the going rate, but be prepared to escalate.

Make sure you are in line with legal requirements once you become an employer:

- Apply for an employer identification number and file additional tax forms.
- You are responsible for withholding her wages for Medicare and Social Security and Federal income taxes plus unemployment.
- Consult with your accountant, attorney, or a service in your community that is set up to help you with everything you need to do and know when you employ household help.

SHE NAMES HER PRICE

"My nanny is tougher than anybody I've had to deal with in business," says Sharon, a marketing executive. "She is very good at getting the money and privileges she wants because she holds the power—our two-year-old son. My husband and I have thought about replacing her, but only for a moment or two. That's because she's good; she's older and sensible and has good judgment.

"A friend gave me great advice: there's only one question—will the woman stand between your kid and a bullet? If you can answer yes, then you give her what she wants."

She Started. Now What?

Give her a list of absolutely everything you want done and exactly how you want it done. You don't have time to explain or answer questions every morning, nor will you always remember everything you want to tell her.

Some of these are things you can talk to a sitter about, such as your philosophy of child-rearing and the kind of care you want. The list you leave should have some greater permanence.

The sitter's must-have list:
- Where to find everything in your house.
- The school and activity calendar.
- Important phone numbers.
- A map of the neighborhood, including all the places she will visit for you, such as the dry cleaner and shoemaker.
- Your own recipes, if she's cooking.
- A list of snacks that are tolerated and those that are taboo.
- How to do the laundry.
- Your medical insurance numbers.
- How many children are allowed to be in your car.
- Bedtimes, snack times, homework times, reading times.
- Exactly how to proceed in the case of an emergency.
- Your children's activities, from lessons to games to play-dates, plus phone numbers and directions to get there.

HOW DO YOU KNOW IF YOU'VE PICKED THE RIGHT PERSON?

Marianne has a method that works for her. "It takes me six weeks," she says. "I give her two weeks to figure out our life, two weeks to confirm my intuition and talk to her about any problems, and then two weeks to fix any difficulties. It works every time. I had hired one sitter who started in August, and everything was just fine. The kids didn't have many obligations,

---

and life was relaxed. But in September our family goes on automatic pilot, and she couldn't handle it. That was it."

Bad things happen to good parents, and sometimes those big surprises will slap you in the face. I arrived home from work one dark, cold winter day to find my eight-month-old son sleeping in his stroller on our front porch (in the middle of a large urban area, mind you). I scooped him up and ran in the house. The oh-so-reliable baby-sitter was in the living room reading a magazine. What could she have been thinking? She thought he needed some fresh air, and she was checking on him every fifteen minutes. (Was she unfamiliar with the concept of pushing a child in a stroller?) End of story. Not really the end. I had a funny twinge about her when she came to us, but I was desperate, and she was good enough, I thought.

Just about everybody has a horror story to tell. Blair and her husband are attorneys, and they hired a live-in nanny to care for their baby. One night they came home and found a different nanny with their son. Their nanny drove in shortly—in their car—and she was drunk. They then learned that she had been leaving their son with nannies all over town while she went drinking and would then drive their car home. "No matter how careful you are," she says, "these women are only human beings with flaws. I will never be surprised again."

Some horror stories are far more subtle. After Alice's sitter had been with the family for some months, she'd start making digs to Alice about her capabilities as a mother. "You know your little boy hates you because you don't spend enough time with him," she told Alice. It was shocking to her, but then she found out from her hairdresser that the sitter had taken her son for a trim of his bangs, sat him on her lap, and insisted the child call her Mommy. Not just inappropriate, but terrifying!

Bottom line: Don't wait for two warning signals. This is your child.

How to Check Up on Your Child Care

- If your child is old enough to tell you, listen.
- Call in and talk to your preschooler on the phone. Establish a code word between the two of you in advance so that the child can say it in front of the sitter, and you can get home.
- If your sitter takes your child to playdates or activities, ask what others think.
- Make surprise visits. It's fair.
- Parents have started to use surveillance equipment— video cameras hidden in clocks, stuffed animals, and lamps. If you suspect you need it, check with a local security company.

IF YOU SUSPECT YOUR SITTER OR NANNY IS STEALING, SET UP A SITUATION THAT TEMPTS HER

Unbeknownst to anyone in her home, Pamela put a ring under a rug, and the nanny took it. "A person who will take a ring has already taken stamps or loose change from you," she says.

And Blair noticed lots of cash missing. Her husband suspected the nanny, and one evening they counted cash together, put it in Blair's wallet, then went down to dinner. "The nanny disappeared for a while, and when we went up to count the cash after dinner, some was missing. I couldn't prove it was our cash—I had no serial numbers—but when I called the agency and told them about it, they sent someone new in two days."

Forget All This: When Can I Leave My Responsible Child Home Alone?

There's the rub in parenthood. You invest all this time and energy just so they can be independent of you. At some point, you'll be able to leave them alone. It's nerve-racking when you first have a latchkey kid.

Of course, it depends on your child, but many working mothers find that by the time a child is nine she's able to be at home alone during daylight hours.

How to make sure your child is safe at home alone:
- Try to arrange for a buddy to walk home from school or from the bus stop with your children.
- Teach your children not to dangle keys before they get in the house.
- Have your children call or page you the minute they come home.
- Ask about their days, and listen to their voices to make sure they're okay.
- Tell them not to answer the phone, but to screen calls on the answering machine.
- Teach your children the alarm code, and have them keep the alarm on when they're home alone.
- Tell them not to answer the door.
- Have something very specific for them to do when they come home, such as homework, then reading. Be sure you get home before the television goes on.
- No playdates without supervision.
- Don't let them use the stove or knives. Have snacks that are already made.
- Find out if there are neighbors at home whom your children can go to in an emergency.
- Don't give newly alone children lots of chores and responsibilities. They have enough on their minds.
- Make sure an adult can be home by six to start dinner. It's upsetting to be home alone too long.

BABY TIP

A sitter can put on a great act for you. A baby has no inhibitions. Trust a baby who screams when a caregiver picks him up.

Make sure your baby is clean, seems well-fed, and is, of course, free of any bruises.

Dealing with Emergencies from Snow Days to Sick Days to the Day Your Pipes Burst

Emergencies like these have nothing to do with an ambulance showing up at your front door, unless you need one for your nervous breakdown when you can't find somebody to stay with the children while you go to work.

HOW TO SHOVEL THROUGH A SNOW DAY

- Have a plan in place before the first flake falls.
- If you can't get to work, forget about it. The problem with finding child care for a snow day is that often a sitter or relative can't get to your house, but you're still supposed to go to work.
- Arrange for a teacher from the nursery school (whose school is also closed) to cover for you. Keep your relationship with her when your children are in elementary school.
- Shuttle kids over to a neighbor's house, either a working mother who's staying home for the day or a stay-at-home mom. Reciprocate by taking her kids on a weekend or on a day she wants to go shopping alone. Bake cookies for her. Offer to pay her. Try not to do this too often.
- Establish a group of working mothers who help one another out on snow days, either by designating one mom to stay home or one house with a live-in nanny who's already going to be there.

- When your kids are old enough to be alone, do phone baby-sit. Keep the alarm on, and have them call you hourly during the day.
- Take your laptop so that you can work at home if you think there's going to be a blizzard overnight. Talk to your supervisor or human resources director about establishing a snow day/sick day policy.

Here's a sample: each employee receives one sick/personal day per month. You also receive five additional sick/personal days to use during the year for obligations to family members.

MANAGING SICK DAYS IS NOTHING TO SNEEZE AT

- Try to stay home and work on the phone.
- Have a list of sitters who are flexible. College students and nurses are particularly good for this. You may need to beg.
- Sometimes you have to take a mildly sick or recovering child to work with you. Pack up a bag of activities: paper, coloring books, markers, crayons, little games, plus lots of snacks and juice, just as if you were going on a car trip.
- Trade off with your spouse.
- Keep in touch with a former baby-sitter and call if you can't find someone.
- Find a child-care center that is established to take only sick children.

Finding suitable child care is going to weigh on your mind for years. You'll alternate between desperation, relief, anxiety, and just plain worry. When it works out perfectly, bathe in its glory.

When my children were still in nursery school, one of the nursery school teachers, who was a college student, would bring them home every afternoon. She was wonderful, but was also graduating. She had a friend who was going to be around for the summer who could help out.

My expectations were rather limited, but when I met Jenny I knew she was a gift. A kind, sweet, resourceful, responsible, and personable high school cheerleader who was also about to go to Harvard Law School. I was bursting to call my sister-in-law, who shares tales of baby-sitting with me. My sister-in-law's response: "Should I be jealous that I'm not her or that I didn't hire her?"

▪ 5 ▪

Going to School to Get an Education for Your Children

When my daughter was in second grade, I parked the car one morning after I dropped the children off to help her bring a project into the classroom. I took a few minutes to talk to her teacher and look at the bulletin boards, and as I left the building to go to my car and off to work, I saw a group of about ten mothers from her class animatedly talking. I gave them a little wave on my way to the car and then changed my mind about getting in. I wanted to know what they were saying, what privileged information and precious gossip they had about the school or the teacher or the children. I walked over and asked casually, "Anything going on I should know about?"

They smiled. "No," they answered. "Not a thing." I had no idea what they were talking about. My daughter made it fine through second grade without my learning what the mothers were ever gossiping about from one day to the next, but being the last to know is how I feel about school.

Getting and interpreting information when you're a working mother is like cracking a spy code. Your children are not the biggest help either. For one, they couldn't even answer what you really want to know, since they think the most important information is about which teacher gives the least homework and what takes place between their friends. A proposed change in a tracking system—portrayed in scientific terms—is not high on their agendas. And, of course, your children don't really want you to be privy to all that information anyway. It's their territory.

Certainly, the territory is yours, too, because you want to make sure your children get the best education possible, and that the teachers know your children and keep you informed. To do that, you have to find out how to get the information you need.

You won't get it exchanging gossip in the parking lot, working at the plant sale, or going on every single field trip. Instead, learn to establish a presence at school, a connection that shows your children how committed you are to what they're doing every single day, that you know it's important and worthwhile.

For your child to be successful at school, you don't have to know every single thing that goes on there. You only have to let the teachers know that you put your children first.

What You Really Need to Know

- Be informed about the issues surrounding education, have opinions, and express them. You don't have to know as much as a school administrator, but you can't make sound judgments without knowing where you stand and what you want for your children.
- Don't base your opinions on the way it was when you went to elementary or high school. You have a selective, not entirely accurate, completely one-sided memory of your own education. Besides, many of today's issues,

from low budgets to high technology were not even issues in your day.

How to do your homework:
- Read the education stories in the morning paper.
- Use the Internet to get information by selecting "education" on your browser.
- Read parenting papers and magazines, which often cover education.
- Know your state and community's policies.
- Know about national math and reading standards, and how your state and school measure up.
- Be informed about what the Secretary of Education thinks.
- Ask for your child's standardized test scores and find out what they mean.
- Ask questions at parents' nights.
- Know about physical education standards at your school.
- Learn about the differences between teaching boys and girls.
- Find out how computers are being used in schools.

Where Is Your Child Going to School?

First of all, nursery school matters. It's not as though you're preparing for the Ivy League, but there are different ways to teach little kids. Some preschools teach little more than writing letters and building blocks, while others have almost a first-grade curriculum. You want cozy? You want strict? It's all out there . . . when you know what you're looking for.
- Do you want your child to learn reading and math before kindergarten?
- Are computer skills important?
- Does your child need an exceptionally long nap time, and will the school accommodate you?
- Do you want your child to take many field trips?

- Are you looking for individualized development?
- Do you want daily progress reports?
- Do you need transportation?

Investigate the preschools in your community. Many of the suggestions below for assessing a school apply to preschool, too. Ask friends, find out where the neighborhood kids go, and, most important—apply early. If you put it off, you'll find yourself without choices. And there goes Harvard.

Schools Are Not All Alike

You may think that nursery school is the only one you will choose before college because you've already determined that your children will be receiving a public school education.

However, you probably choose your community based on its schools, but your community may not automatically send elementary school graduates straight to the neighborhood middle school.

Some school systems now offer the students a choice for middle school and high school, based on their academic or artistic strengths. Or for a reason unknown to you at this very moment, you may make the decision to put your child into private school.

What should you think about when you choose a school? These suggestions apply from 1 + 1 to quantum physics.

- What do you want the school to do? (Teach the basics, give a moral structure, provide multiethnic culturization, offer artistic enrichment and a center for all activities, encourage academic challenge and socialization, are a few examples.)
- What's the population of the school?
- What's the average class size?

- What kinds of teachers does the school hire?
- What are the academic goals?
- How are they measured?
- Is there tracking and how does it work?
- Learn about the writing, reading, math, social studies, science, and physical education programs.
- How do computers fit into the curriculum? Is the school on-line?
- How much outside reading is required?
- Do students write for every subject?
- When and which languages are taught?
- What is the artistic curriculum? (Art, music, dance, musical instruments?)
- How are the students measured for success?
- Ask to see a sample report card.
- How is the contact managed between parents and the school?
- What's the discipline policy?
- How are emergencies handled?
- How can the parents be involved in the school?
- Are there family events?
- Are the children involved in community service?
- How much fund-raising has to be done?

Staying Involved

Talking to the teacher about your child's progress, then helping your child with homework are all the involvement you really need to have.

You're going to get a note every September, though, asking you which volunteer activities you'll be doing. These are no longer the exclusive province of at-home mothers, but if you don't have an inch in your schedule to jam one more thing into it, that is just fine. Throw out the note, and when you have time to come back to the concept of helping out, the school will welcome you.

About some things, you have no choice.

Events you must not miss and rules you must not break:
- Go to parent night.
- Go to parent/teacher conferences.
- If you can't make the class meetings, call another mom to find out what went on.
- Go to PTA meetings.
- Go to the class plays and performances. If you absolutely can't make it, send your spouse, a grandparent, an aunt or uncle or cousin or best friend who will take pictures. And be sure to tell your child in advance who's coming.
- Pick up, or have the caregiver pick up, your children on time after school. It's embarrassing for them when they're always the last ones waiting, not to mention that they feel pretty low on your list of priorities.
- Pick up the unwritten culture of the school. If every mother volunteers at the annual book sale, you better find thirty minutes a year to sell *The Cat in the Hat*.
- Know when your child has to have something special for a field trip, a play, or a project. Nobody likes to be the only one who isn't prepared.
- Go to field day.
- Go to your child's athletic events.

IT'S NOT THE WORST THING IN THE WORLD

When my son was in first grade I missed the parents' day. Rationally, I know it was because we had moved and hadn't received the notice in the mail, and I probably wasn't paying very close attention to notes in his book bag. He got over it more quickly than I did.

TALKING TO A TEACHER ABOUT YOUR DIVORCE

Though half of marriages end in divorce, all children are affected by it. It helps your child when the teacher knows what kind of home life your child has. Suzanne decided to be very open with her daughter's teacher. "My eleven-year-old daughter was crying in class, and I had to do something," says Suzanne. "I encouraged her to talk to her counselor, then I talked to the counselor and told her to pick up the phone anytime to call me."

Joanne, who keeps medical records in a large hospital, divorced when her children were five and nine. "I talked to both of their teachers," says Joanne, "and the little one seemed to be okay. My son, the older child, however, is like a tree that grew bent. If I weren't putting in so much time in my job, I'd be concentrating on him. I worry because I was a troubled adolescent and ran away from home. I don't want that to happen to him. His teacher was so glad I enlightened her. 'We should be on the same wavelength,' she told me. That really relaxed me."

The Teachers Are Your Best Connection to School

Establish a relationship with the teacher. If you have an elementary school child, it's easy to know whom to meet. By middle and high school, start with the homeroom teacher. Just introduce yourself, and you'll have an association with each other. If you need to connect with a math or science teacher later in the year, then do it.

Arrange a meeting at the beginning of the year. How early? Well, you know how school always starts on a Thursday or Friday? Be in there the following Monday morning. This avoids getting into a paper relationship with the teacher so that if any issues arise the teacher can pick up the phone and talk to someone she or he actually knows. Also, the teacher should know you through eyes other than your children's. It helps the teacher know where your kids are coming from.

Rather than a chat session, have a list of things to talk about when meeting your child's new teacher:

- Go in with objectives you have for your child in the coming year.
- Talk about any weaknesses your child has.
- Talk about any learning disabilities such as dyslexia.
- Tell the teacher about your child's special interests.
- Discuss areas of strength, both academic and personal.
- Be very specific about areas that need attention, and give examples.
- Ask about structuring the homework environment and how much you need to be involved.
- Tell the teacher about your career and how much you travel for business. He or she might want to know when you're away because some children react to it.
- Emphasize that you are always available to talk about your child.

TAKE TIME TO MAKE TIME

Vernel, a single mother who always had very little time as an entrepreneur running a temp service, always touched base with the teacher at the beginning of the year. "I found working hand-in-hand was much better. We trusted each other, and I always made pop-in visits during the school year. Not everybody knows you can do that, but you learn a lot more than at those scheduled parent conferences when they're ready for you."

Going to Bat for Your Child

How far do you go? If you had to answer that right now, you'd say you'd go to Mars, to the core of the Earth, or circle it a hundred times. Working mothers tend to feel a little guiltier if a conflict comes up and can be quite savvy about bringing certain skills from the workforce into play when they do battle with the school.

How to stick up for your child so that you get results:

- Give a situation some time. Things often work themselves out. Kids will start to get along, or your child will grasp a math concept.
- Deal with a crisis such as violence or cheating immediately.
- Go to the teacher first. Explain the situation and what you want done about it.
- Go to the principal next, and go again if nothing changes.
- Make sure the school representatives hear what you are saying.
- Listen very carefully to what they are saying.
- After it's resolved, arrange to follow up regularly, but diminish its importance in your mind.
- Understand that the school has your child's best interests at heart. If you don't feel it, you need to move your child to another school.

IN TEACHERS WE TRUST

Ruth, a human resources director, often travels on business and knows she isn't good about keeping track of school. So when her fourth-grade daughter was having a difficult year, she thought it was only because her daughter didn't like the teacher. "It seemed to me she was complaining about the teacher picking on her," says Ruth, "and I didn't know how serious it was. I thought it was just a personality conflict because the year before

---

the teacher told us that if all children were like my daughter, her life would be heaven.

"In April, the school called and asked to see my husband and me. They suggested we go into family therapy. I was shocked, but we did it, and it turned out that our daughter wanted more attention. She hated that I was traveling so much. Of course, I beat myself up about it. If I had been around I would have been more aware and I would have done something myself. I'm just glad the school found it."

You Really Can Manage Homework When You're Not Home

Some children go to after-school programs, some go to a baby-sitter, some go to activities, some have lessons, some come home alone. And not one of them really wants to do homework as soon as they walk through the door. That's why you have to instill the homework ethic right from the beginning.

Homework rules:
- Have a snack, then do homework—all of it.
- No television until homework is finished.
- No social phone calls until homework is finished.
- If your children have playdates, they do their homework together first, then play.
- Designate a regular place to work, whether it's at your child's desk or at the kitchen table.
- If your children have homework questions, ask the baby-sitter, go on-line for one of the teacher/homework assistance services, or call you.
- Call a homework buddy if your school has this program. Older elementary children are teamed up with a middle-school buddy who can answer questions.

- A parent should check the homework of a little kid and go over the homework of the bigger kid every night.
- Assignment books must be available for the perusal of the parent at any time.

TRY TO BE AVAILABLE WHEN YOUR CHILDREN CALL YOU AT WORK WITH HOMEWORK PROBLEMS

Shelly's son called one day when she had a meeting going on in her office. "He was hysterical," she remembers, "because he couldn't figure out rounding up and rounding down. I took the call and taught him how to do it while I was sitting in the meeting."

School Won't Take Care of Everything: How to Help Your Child Be Prepared

Is it organization time for the children? Are they turning into us with date books and notes and little sticky papers on everything? Almost.

If you teach a child to put his toys away, you should certainly teach him the skills to be a better, more efficient student.

FIVE THINGS YOU NEED TO GIVE A STUDENT

1. **Supplies.** Use your own organizational skills to show your child how to divide up folders and notebooks by subject, how to label them and put papers into them as soon as they can. Then decide together the supplies: folders, notebooks, pencils, pens, erasers, ruler, pencil sharpener, scissors, glue stick, tape, assignment book, crayons, markers, dictionary, and loose-leaf paper. Check in regularly to ensure your child has plenty of everything.

A TIP ON NOTEBOOKS

Organizing papers into different file folders may look like a good idea, but think again. What happens when those folders fall out of the book bag? The papers go flying everywhere. You may even have to pick them up. Instead, file all the papers by dividers in a three-ring binder, encased in nylon with a big zipper around the outside. It drops. So what?

---

2. **Book bag.** This is the traveling office. Check it frequently, and act on the notes you find in there. Help your child clean it out every few weeks.

3. **Reading list.** Yes, you want your child to read, but it happens a lot easier if you set goals together. Make it the amount of time spent or number of pages or number of books, whatever is most comfortable for your child's level. Then talk about the books together.

4. **Time to learn math facts.** Eventually, the whole world will be using calculators constantly, and we won't even have to know how to divide. Today, we still have to drill children on those facts. Set a goal for learning the facts, either by date, by numbers completed, or by functions learned. Give a reward.

5. **Unconditional support.** If you see that your child is faltering in a subject—even a tiny bit—fix it immediately. Hire a tutor. The private (or semiprivate) assistance your child receives is invaluable. Make sure the tutor communicates with the teacher.

How to Take the Next Step
Beyond Your Own Child: Volunteering

Just as schools are getting much better about holding meetings at 7:30 A.M. or P.M., so, too, are they improving in establishing off-hours for volunteering. They also can suggest things for you to do that take little time, fit in with a flexible schedule, or center around your skills and interests.

There isn't any working mother who couldn't use her career skills to benefit her children's school.

VOLUNTEERING NEXT TO STAY-AT-HOME MOMS

After the first day of school, Margo, who's a property manager of a retirement community, unpacked her daughter's book bag and found a list of twenty projects she could work on during the school year. "Not one of them was after five P.M.," recalls Margo. "Why do they have to do it during the day? When I said I wanted to be involved, a mother told me, 'This is not a clique. We need help with bake sales and decorating pumpkins.' Sure, but you have to pick up the pumpkin at 1:30 P.M."

One evening Martha got a call from a room mother asking if Martha could be at school between two and three P.M. the next day to make dinosaurs. "She said, 'Since you never do anything for David, you might want to be here,'" says Martha. "I had already gotten over the years of crying because I didn't know the other mothers, so I told her, 'You could really hurt someone's feelings by saying something like that,' but she was oblivious that she had said anything. I have learned to let go of other people's assessments of what kind of mother I am. I have given myself room to be who I am, and I get into the energy of my kids. At least once a year I do something at school."

Face it, ladies. Some mothers have put their careers on hold while they spend a few years with their children. They are the ones who now have the time to schedule pumpkin picking in the middle of the day. There's no reason to waste the time or emotion in battling at-home moms nor to feel unwelcome or unwanted at school. There are many things you can do.

Ask Yourself These Questions
Before You Answer That Questionnaire from School

- Who do you want to be at school?
- Do you want to be involved behind the scenes or with your children?
- How much time can you really give?
- What do your children want you to do? They won't keep it a secret.
- Do you want to use your career skills or your mom skills?
- Can you get away from work during the day?
- Are you more comfortable volunteering at night?
- Do you want to see your child and friends and teachers in action?
- Do you worry that if you don't volunteer your child will be shortchanged?

PICK AN ACTIVITY
- Go on one field trip a year.
- Arrange a field trip to your office.
- Give an hour to a class to talk about what you do. Have plenty of props.
- Help write a grant.
- Work on the school newsletter to parents.
- Bake (don't sell) for the bake sale.
- Serve hot dogs at the football game.
- Be a snow-chain mom and make the 6:30 A.M. calls when school is canceled.
- Send in snacks and supplies for class parties.
- Take a lunch hour to be an art mom. Bring in pictures of famous paintings, then have the kids do an art project.
- Be a science mom. Help the science teacher with a project or nature walk.

- Work at nighttime silent auctions or fund-raisers if you were going to attend anyway. You don't have to do the preparation.
- Make reminder calls for events and projects to other parents during the evening.
- Give a faculty workshop one evening if you have expertise in science, finance, health care, elder care, creative writing, art, or anything else your teachers might need to know more about.
- Teach keyboarding (formerly known as typing) in a computer class.
- Watch kids in the playground at lunchtime.
- Read to kids in the library before school or at lunch.
- Whenever you're asked, send in for the mitten drive, can drive, sweater drive, coat drive.
- Take kids one evening to deliver the donations.

YOUR CHILDREN KNOW
WHAT THEY WANT YOU TO DO

Some children would love to see you on the bus for every field trip, some would be mortified, and some don't care whether you make the Herculean effort. After Caroline learned that her daughter needed more attention, she talked with her about doing work for the school. Her daughter replied, "No! You'd only be involved with the other parents, not me."

Shelly read her high school daughter as one who wanted to keep her mother at arm's length from the school. She understood and accepted it. Her high profile as an advertising executive could be intimidating to a daughter finding herself, so whenever she went to school, Shelly knew to go as Mom. When her daughter asked her to be a speaker to the girls at school about women and careers, which Shelly does often for women's groups and for women in her own company,

---

Shelly said no. "My daughter's face fell," she recalls. "I didn't know it meant so much to her, so I changed my answer and had a wonderful time talking with the girls. Of course, I didn't escape their penetrating questions such as 'When you work do you miss your kids?' We were both glad I did this, and I had never imagined it as something I could do for my daughter and her school."

Playing Hooky

We're going to hope no teachers are reading this part because here we're talking about breaking the rules. If you have a kid who's obsessed with perfect attendance, forget it. But it's nice to take an occasional mental health day—a personal day as it's called in the human resources world—to be with your children.

Sally, who's an attorney in St. Louis, loved to go to school at noon on opening day of the baseball season, tell the secretary that her children had dentist appointments, and then take them to the Cardinals game. Her daughter caught the spirit, too, and once when she called Sally to pick her up early because she was sick, Sally asked, "You're not really sick, are you?"

"Sort of," she answered. "I missed my sandbox." So they went home together and played in the sandbox.

Hannah schedules a special day off from school with each of her three children during the year. "A day alone when you know you should be somewhere else is really exciting," she says. "We plan an activity like going to a museum or a movie, not errands, not anything we might do during a Saturday time together."

It's special and precious to have time just to be

together, to talk or keep silent, to feel the rhythm of your children, and have a sense of who they are becoming. When you get the note from school that your child has a half day off coming up, take the half day together. This is the kind of time you're looking for.

■ 6 ■

Planning Activities:
Your Guide to Building the Résumé

Activities are a huge indication of the seismic change in the way kids and families operate. When I was growing up, a kid would come home to play with me after school, call up her mom to say where she was, and, unless she was missing her piano lesson, that was it. No such ease today. Now children are committed in all kinds of after-school activities, living highly structured, planned, and arranged lives. The birthday party schedule is nothing; activities are the events that fill up your family calendar.

You better stay on top of this one.

By the time you learn that the deadline for putting your little alley-ooper into the premier basketball league is nigh, you can be sure you're late already and that you're going to be begging the director of the league to put your kid on a team. And always remember: the most desirable violin teacher never has openings.

But the graven image of the saintly soccer mom notwith-standing (Where's the respect for the hockey mom, the rid-ing mom, the swim-meet mom, the theater mom, or the ballet mom who also drives, cheers, and provides ample snacks?), activities are a major part of your child's social life. And learning to play on a team or throw a pot aren't such bad skills either. You'll certainly find yourself participating, especially in the tremendous effort and skill it takes to find the right activity, then getting your child there and home.

Another nightmarish time for you is called summer vaca-tion, when there is no regularly scheduled activity from early morning to midafternoon, and you have to find it. Anyone for year-round school?

Activities Start Early

I am a believer in putting this off as long as possible, but when I took my one-year-old son to a play group, he was the only one who was enrolled in only one activity. I still had a bag in the attic filled with mementos I was meaning to put into a baby book some day, and these moms had their kids in movement, music, art, and gymnastics classes—and all their photos in albums. Way ahead of me.

The easy way to have a toddler student:
- Have your children attend classes on your day off, whether it's a Saturday or a weekday if you have a more flexible schedule. Don't even think about finding the energy to do this after work.
- One activity a week is plenty.
- Read the bulletin board in the pediatrician's office to find out what classes are available.
- Call your local Y. There are great classes from baby swim (it's fun) to music and exercise.
- Your local parenting paper will probably have a schedule in August or September of available classes. Call a few

that sound interesting, and try to visit the facility.
- Try to connect with one kind, experienced mother who will guide you.
- Sign up for as few classes as possible in case it's not working out.
- You might be happier in a Mommy and Me class rather than in a Nanny and Me class. Check to find out who's in the class.
- Location is important. Your child is way too little for you to travel a long distance for a particular teacher. You'll have plenty of time for that later.

By the time your children are ready to take part in after-school and weekend activities, you'll have an idea of what may interest them. They, however, will need your help to direct them. And because you're not plugged into all the other mothers, you're going to have to do some research yourself.

Try these criteria for finding the right activities:
- One physical thing (sports).
- One artsy thing (music, art, chess, crafts, dance, science, for example).
- One buddy thing (scouting, 4-H).
- Look for fun and a future direction your child may want to take.

YOU THOUGHT YOU KNEW YOUR CHILDREN?

We can have crazy notions about the potential of our children—of the musical, artistic, dramatic, and athletic abilities they possess. I mistook my son's interest in a friend who handcrafted violins as a burning desire to play one himself. I enrolled him in the Suzuki method (in which Mother also takes violin lessons) when he was only four. He might have wanted to play, but he surely didn't embrace the notion of practicing. I really

---

didn't want to battle a small child nor stamp out his interest in music, so we quit. Turns out he still doesn't want to play an instrument. Be sure it is the interest of your child, not your own frustrations and desires, that directs you.

Interests can change, too. My daughter wanted to ride horses desperately. So I would drive her forty-five minutes on freezing dark winter afternoons way out into the country to the stables, while I sat in the car for another forty-five minutes reading or tapping out something on my laptop, then drove the next forty-five minutes home. Then I made dinner. I wasn't exactly crazy about this routine, so when we moved very close to a stable, I was quite happy and very ready to take her. No! She had changed her mind and now hated riding. We're on to flute lessons and chorus. Be flexible.

What to Consider When You Consider After-School Activities

- What does your child like to do most?
- In what areas does your child show most aptitude?
- What kind of budget can you allocate for these classes? They can add up quickly.
- What supplies does your child need, and are they readily available?
- How is your child going to get there and then home?
- Who are the other children participating?
- What are the ages of the other children in the class? Make sure your child is in an age-appropriate group. Some kids are great with an older group; others need to be with their own age; many don't like to be with younger children.
- Who's sponsoring the activity? Investigate the reputation of the teacher or organization.

- Where is it taking place?
- When will your child be able to do his homework?
- Will they get a snack at the activity or do they have to bring their own?
- Do classes continue during winter and spring vacation, and is there the opportunity for more involvement during vacations?
- Are you going to get a chance to see what your child has accomplished? Is there a performance, an art show, or awards ceremony?
- What's the nature of parent involvement? Do you really have the time, or can you make it available?

Just as with programs for very young children, it's best not to sign up for a full year of lessons. Take the shortest amount of time—usually a trimester or semester—then evaluate the activity, the particular place your child takes it, and how much your child likes it.

WHAT'S AVAILABLE?

There is everything imaginable—and even that which you had no idea existed. My daughter and her friend were making pillows out of old shorts. They sewed the legs and tops closed after stuffing them with old T-shirts, but it didn't dawn on me to find a sewing class for my daughter. Her friend's mother had the brainstorm, then searched until she found someone who would teach little girls, and they've loved the classes they've taken together.

Today you can find so much for your child to do after school. Classes are offered for the kindergartner up to a twelfth grader. No more waiting for the high school chess club if you're a six-year-old whiz.

How a Frazzled Working Mother
Gathers the Information

- Go to parent coffees and PTA meetings and ask what other kids are doing.
- Ask your child's teacher for some guidance, especially a teacher whose field is one in which your child shows aptitude.
- Call the local Y.
- Read the parenting paper for articles about different activities, and call the reporter who wrote the story. That person has been paid to do the research and can be very helpful.
- Read all the notices that come home with your child from school and religious classes. A lot of information is right in your house.
- Call your child's best friend's mother and try to coordinate activities.
- It's best to visit a facility to see if it has the right environment and teaching method.
- After you've enrolled your child, take him once and talk to the other mothers who are hanging around. They often know a lot about other things going on as well as additional places to take the same kind of class.
- Realize that you might make a few mistakes until you get into the right network of mothers.
- Ask the director of the organization or individual teacher for names of parents you can call. Word of mouth is definitely the more trustworthy way to learn about a program than ads or brochures.

WHAT'S OVERPROGRAMMING?

You hear about this all the time. Understanding what is too much for your child is up to you. It seems to me that if a young child never has a day to come home, close the door to his room and be by himself, or to run outside and play, things have gotten out of hand. Make sure your child has some time during the week that can be his very own time to do nothing or to choose to have a playdate.

No child is strong enough to withstand the pressures of constant programming. If your child is on the road to learning, then mastering, an art, she has to want it more than anything. Expertise takes many hours of practice, and you'll have to be supportive and understanding of the commitment so that she is able to have time for homework and friends. And always be attuned to signs of cracking.

Some parents love the idea of many activities. They feel that it keeps children from turning into bored, trouble-seeking teenagers. Joyce owned a ballet school in the Los Angeles area when her children were growing up. She kept them busy after school because she wanted her children to have many interests and not turn to drugs. "My husband and I never saved a dime," she says. "We spent it all on the kids for lessons, classes, and camps. We sent them to every lesson you can imagine to find out what they did best. I never wanted to crush their creativity." Nevertheless, these were activities the children *wanted* to do.

Joyce saw another side of the excesses of activity, too: parents with misplaced ambitions. "We had auditions in which mothers could watch their children through two-way mirrors. I could never stand in the room and listen to the way they were judging their children or complaining that they weren't getting a fair chance. All the jealousy and back-biting of stage mothers makes it a lot less fun." Think before you push.

Are the Other Working Mothers Driving Carpools?

Most working mothers don't drive carpools. Sometimes a baby-sitter, nanny, or grandparent does it for them. There are other alternatives; you have to be creative.

The best ways to get there and back if you can't do it yourself:
- Make sure transportation arrangements are in place before the activity begins.
- Investigate the activities available right at your child's school. Don't discount the value of after-school programs.
- Sign up with your child's best friend. The other mother is most likely one you can negotiate and trade favors with easily.
- If there is transportation for a fee, *always* sign up for it.
- If you find a mom who will drive *to* the class, volunteer to be the mom who *always* picks up.
- Find a college student (through the college-placement office or baby-sitting service) who drives and will take your child.
- Keep in touch with your child's preschool teachers. Some are looking for extra money and will drive your child.
- If the class is along your child's school-bus route, see whether the driver can make a special stop. Don't forget this favor at Christmas time.
- Familiarize your child with your community's public transportation. By the time you have a middle schooler, you can feel pretty confident if she travels with another child.
- If it's available, sign up for an activity at a facility that has after-care, so you can pick up your child at 6:30 if necessary.

PRACTICING, HATING IT, DROPPING OUT

When Allison's twins started second grade, she enrolled them in piano lessons. She had met a mother in their class who taught piano, and they could walk to her house after school for lessons. Allison was worried they would never practice, since she wasn't home at the critical after-school time every day to make sure they did.

"I didn't want to come home and nag them about practicing," she says, "so after we were finished with dinner, I'd always say, 'Please play for Mommy while I do the dishes. It would make it so much more pleasant.' I felt much better about it. No arguments." And it's a relationship that emphasizes pride and self-respect. When you come home after a long day, you don't want to yell at your children.

After six years, Allison's children had had enough and wanted to quit. "I didn't really want them to quit because they were decent at it, and I knew they'd be sorry when they were adults. So I told them to take off one year. They did and now play more willingly. If we had screamed through it, I know it wouldn't have worked."

Mothering an Athlete

We never had all these organized sports as kids either. But we never had the emphasis on physical fitness that we have now.

A big reason so much of this happens outside of the school day is that many school systems are forced to cut their budgets, and phys ed can fall to the bottom of the list. Your children can wind up having gym just once a week. We have to take responsibility for finding phys ed for our children.

Team or Individual Sports?

. art out with one of each—soccer and swimming, for example. You won't know if your child is a team player until he's on a team. Some children are thrilled by the competition, others are belittled by it.

Choosing your sport:
- What does your child like? What would be fun?
- What is your child ready for? What kind of skills does he or she have?
- What does your community offer?
- What are all your child's friends doing?
- Does your school offer an after-school program your child can do easily?
- How involved do parents have to be in this sport? You'd be amazed. Duties range from coaching to cleanup to snacks to phoning to accounting to managing to newsletter writing.
- How much does it cost to be in the sport?
- Do you have to buy the equipment?
- When are the games?
- When are the practices?
- Do you have to travel far to the competitions? Many swimming moms will tell you stories about driving two hours to a meet, watching their child compete for two minutes, then driving back. Hockey moms leave home at five A.M. most Saturdays during the winter. Riding moms travel far and wide to horse shows. Your child has to love it.

Go to the Games

- Put all the games, meets, matches, competitions, and awards banquets on your family calendar. Then figure out how many you or your husband or your relatives can get to.

- For events during the week, skip your normal lunch hour and leave early.
- There is no reason to be at every class or watch every practice or lesson. In fact, your child will hate your scrutinizing her every move. Don't feel guilty if you have somebody else take your child to practices (see the suggestions for after-school activities), but do your best to get to the competitions, when your child is ready and eager to be noticed.
- An advantage of being at the games is that when you sit among other parents with a common goal of cheering the team, it's very easy to strike up a conversation and become acquainted with them. You'll also meet your child's friends and have an enlightening glimpse of your child relating to others.

I'll Be There, But Is Any of This Taking Us to College?

If you're talking about lots of scholarship money from a Big Ten school and thinking of watching your little boy play football on television on Saturday afternoons, well, you know his talents and commitment have to be extraordinary. On the other hand, many high school guidance counselors have become quite savvy about sports that can lead to college placement and money.

When your child is in middle school, you can think more seriously about harnessing spectacular talents. Many middle-school and high-school coaches and guidance counselors are prepared to present options to parents. Also, they often advise looking at growing or offbeat sports like lacrosse and fencing, then matching up the college with your children's sports and academic strengths.

WHAT HAPPENS WHEN SPORTS AREN'T FUN ANYMORE?

You might not even notice it, especially if you were never involved in sports. The anger or depression might just seem to you like stages of growing up that you have to deal with. Cynthia had a very close look at the perils of sports through the eyes of her three children.

Her oldest is a girl who is very athletic. "We knew that sports were a great way to get money for college scholarships," says Cynthia, "so we pushed her toward volleyball and basketball, which were both offered in community programs. She did very well and got a $4,000 scholarship. With our son, we turned to football. My husband has ties to football, and he was very good about arranging car pools, buying equipment, and getting to more games than I did.

"Our son started in midget football, was quite good, and was always voted captain of his team. As he was getting older, we knew that his talent could take him far, so we looked at a local private school that has a great reputation for athletics and sending its football players to excellent colleges. He was able to get a scholarship there.

"We were all proud of him, but it meant even more to my husband, who had always wanted to go to this private school himself. Our son got up very early every morning to get to school, which was far from our home, and he came home very late after football practice. When he was home, all he did was sleep. It didn't feel right to me. By the end of October, I recognized it as a downward spiral of depression. I talked to my son, who told me he was unhappy because he loved the new school's athletics but didn't have time to make friends. He missed his old school and his old friends. I saw no need for him to be so upset. I knew exactly what to do. I told him that we weren't going to tell his father just yet, but that we were going to pull him out and re-enroll him in his old school. He was so relieved. When it was all set, and he'd finished his last Friday, I told my husband our son was going back to the old school. He was taken aback, but he understood."

His best friend, though, didn't fare so well. He'd also played midget football, but knew he wasn't as talented. He had a brother who was interested in music and longed to be part of a band, but felt that his parents were pushing him hard toward football. "We had his parents over to talk to them about it, but they were too wrapped up in it. It was their whole social life, too, and they didn't want him to drop out. Finally, he did quit, and his father took the team pictures and certificates of merit off the walls. The kid dyed his hair green and got all kinds of piercings. He doesn't speak to his father."

Cynthia's third child chose not to do sports at all.

Warning Signs of a Stressed-Out, Overpushed Athlete

- Endless excuses not to go to practice or games.
- Frequent injuries.
- Constant negative comparisons to successful athletes in the peer group and worries that he can't make the grade.

When you hear any of these, sit down and talk to your child. Tell him it's okay to quit. Let him know you love him no matter what.

How About After-School Programs?

These can be your lifesaver. If you can get there by five P.M., that is. Why is it that a school imagines it's doing working mothers such a favor and then ends the program every day before work is over?

The best after-school programs:
- Offer transportation
- Are at your child's school
- Start out every afternoon with playtime
- Have a variety of activities from sports to arts
- Provide snacks
- Have homework supervision in a quiet area
- Encourage you to let your child just play at least one afternoon a week
- End at 6:30 P.M.
- Are in session all day during school vacations

Living with That New-Fangled Invention: The Playdate

One of the activities you don't want your children to miss is the ubiquitous playdate. For a working mother, these can be quite complicated to arrange.

Preschoolers thrive on playdates. To participate, you have to have a sitter who drives or can otherwise transport your little one (by stroller or public transportation) to other homes. Or wait until the weekends.

How to make playdates happen:
- Take the initiative. Ask your child who she wants to play with, then call.
- Give up a Saturday morning with your child so that she can play with someone. It's important to have those out-of-school experiences together.
- When you pick up your child, or the other child's parent picks him up, engage the mom in conversation. You're more likely to work things out with another parent if you have a sense of who she is.
- For after-school playdates, let your sitter handle the logistics.

- Arrange with the school-bus driver to bring your child's friend home.
- Sometime when you have an afternoon off, have your child invite a friend to come along on an outing.
- Forget the after-school playdate, and do weekend sleep-overs instead.

Suddenly, It's Summer

The appearance of the first crocus signals the beginning of the summer-camp hunt. The articles about summer activities, the camp fairs, the camp directors' visits to your home town, the applications to join your community pool, and the endless flyers about hurrying to book your child's summer fun all come to you in February and March.

CAMPS AND SCHOOLS HAVE
A TON OF SUMMER PROGRAMS

The information is there but not always easy to find. "There is a whole stream of information I have to fight to get," laments Phyllis, who knows few other mothers. "I know I only get bits of it." If that's how you feel, too, rest assured you're not alone. Most working mothers gulp before they plan their children's summers, and then hope for the best in June.

Discovering Day Camp

- Investigate the possibilities at your children's school.
- Check with your community to see the kinds of programs (and transportation) they offer.
- Call local science and art museums, which often have weeklong camps.

- See whether your church or synagogue has a program.
- Call private schools in your area, which have camps for all children.
- Go to a camp fair, and talk to the director, counselors, and campers.
- Find out where your child's good friends are going. Don't wait for your child to find out. Call the other parents yourself.
- Learn where the other children in your neighborhood are going. This helps with car pools.
- Enroll your child in a scouting or 4-H camp if they're already involved.
- Ask about programs at the local Y.
- If your child has a particular interest (music, arts, science, computers), ask the teachers if they know of camps. Often they're counselors at them.
- Call local colleges, which often have day camps and special sports programs.
- If you have an athlete, call your local professional sports teams and ask about summer programs.

YOUR DUTIES FOR DAY CAMP

Once your child is enrolled, you've arranged for transportation (camps are very helpful about this since the children are from all different areas), gotten those medical forms in (make your appointment for a checkup as soon as possible), and bought enough T-shirts and bathing suits so you then won't have too much to do each morning. Day camps are much more of a blur than school.

Have fun. Nevertheless, you don't get off scot-free.

- Have the day's clean towel, dry bathing suit, and sunscreen and hat ready at the door before you go to bed.
- Go to parents' day.
- Read the notices that come home so that you know when it's Backwards Day, Pirate Day, or Dress Like the Counselor Day, and your child can be ready for it.

When Is It Time for Sleep-Away Camp?

The typical seven-year-old is not beating down the door to go to sleep-away camp. Kids that young don't spend the summer at camp unless they have friends, cousins, or older brothers or sisters at the camp. It's very frightening for most children to leave home for eight weeks. Think seriously about sending your child with a best friend or relatives. Even if they're not bunking together, it helps to see a familiar face.

EIGHT WHOLE WEEKS?

You might get to an in-between time when your children feel too old for day camp and too terrified to go away for the whole summer. I faced it when my children were nine and eleven, and I lucked into a two-week program at the Y for children in that age range.

Liz is a very busy real estate agent whose hours are erratic, long, and intense. When her young daughter wanted to go away to camp, Liz found a great summer-long solution that lessened the homesickness and the exorbitant fees many camps charge. Her daughter is a Girl Scout and was able to go away for a week at a time. The girls were dropped at camp every Sunday evening and picked up every Friday evening to go home for the weekend. Liz got to have her crazy work schedule, and her daughter had a great summer.

The non-eight-week camp:
- Check into local camps with four- and two-week sessions.
- Call your local Y about weeklong camps.
- Some special camps (sports or science camps) have one-week sessions.
- Scouting camps are flexible about sessions.

EIGHT WHOLE WEEKS!

Not every mother can admit that she's looking forward to the time the children go away. Yet many psychiatrists will tell you that June is the time of greatest stress—not the holiday season. Parents are torn between missing their children and the guilt about wanting them to leave.

For Sally, camp couldn't come soon enough. "When my daughter was little, I dreamed about it," she says. "I thought it would be so nice to be just a couple again and to go out on the spur of the moment. Now that our daughter goes away for eight weeks, it is great, and she has a wonderful time, too."

It's a relief for you when they're away because you don't have to rush home, you don't have to prepare a proper meal every evening, you can run around the house in your underwear (or less), you can work late, you can forget about that big calendar in the kitchen, and you can spend Saturday morning in bed (alone or otherwise).

No Matter How Long Camp Is, You Still Have to Pack

- Start shopping as soon as you get the list.
- If you need uniforms, send for them as soon as possible.
- It sounds ridiculous, but pay the insane fee to have the name tags sewn on for you.
- Find a store that caters to campers. The staff will help you buy, pack, and ship everything.
- Do an inventory in April to see whether last year's stuff fits.
- Have your child watch you put things in the trunk so he knows what color his towels are and what his soap dish looks like.
- Get everything on the list, even if you think your child won't need it.

- Pack bug repellent.
- Take control, and don't leave it up to your child.
- Set aside two atomic weekends for shopping, labeling, and packing if you have to do it yourself.
- Get it done early.

DO YOU HAVE A CHILD WHO DOESN'T LIKE CAMP?

I actually do. It didn't start out that way. He started at day camp when he was five. In fact, I was kind of hoping that he would go to the same camp for a hundred years, but my son developed other interests and didn't have loyalty to his first camp. (I didn't understand because I was one who would have sacrificed a body part for my camp.) He wanted to mix things up a bit. In case you never noticed, every kid does not fit neatly into a preprogrammed slot.

There were enough options around so that one year we added a week of soccer camp, then he went to day camp. Another year he had a week of basketball camp, a week of baseball camp, and four weeks of day camp. One year we tried sports camp, and he absolutely hated it. I hadn't done the research, and I didn't know in advance that the atmosphere was extremely competitive, and I didn't arrange for one of his friends to sign up until much too late. Yes, I took him out of camp, and my summer consisted of days off, baby-sitters on, and lots more television than I would have liked. My daughter likes camp, but she's gone to many, depending on her interests and where her friends were going.

So is everybody organized, booked, planned, enrolled, and signed up? And have you managed to put in some downtime? I was just reminded of it when I was going over my daughter's schedule for fourth grade. "Wow, " I told her, "for the first time ever, you're going to have only one day free after school."

She looked at me seriously. "Mom," she told me, "I can't handle it."

We'll discuss it.

▦ 7 ▦

Taking the Trouble Out of Travel

So how do you really feel when you hear you have to go on a business trip?

Complacent? Hardly.

Anxious is more like it. As much fun as it might be to leave your routine, visit places you never thought you'd get to, have your very own hotel room, rack up zillions of airline miles, and enjoy all-expenses-paid living, it sure is easier when you don't have kids.

As a Mom You Have Two Kinds of Pressures Operating

First, there's the career pressure of impending face time. Nobody goes on a business trip to sit in a hotel and talk on the phone. You're going because some client or business prospect or associate or adversary or sales force needs to see you in person. Traveling means you're about to go on stage as the best representative who could be sent.

Then there's the good old Mom guilt. The kids at home don't really want you to go away, you know, and the notion of your leaving them well cared for and covered for all contingent disasters may be comforting only to you. And no matter what you tell them, no thinking human being will believe that a trip could be all work and no play. The charm of compensatory gifts like little bottles of lovely scented creams and shoe shine mitts wears off quickly.

No wonder you need some guidance to get you through the travails of travel. When we're back from the business trip, we'll go on vacation. I promise.

Deciding Whether It's Necessary

No matter what you hear about business travel—that it's being supplanted by teleconferencing, diminished by electronic communication, or downsized by budgetary restrictions—it's still taking place in a big way. There are sales meetings and conferences and conventions, big meetings, small meetings, plus old-fashioned attention that must be paid to key contacts.

Business travel is often what separates the men from the women and creates the impenetrable glass ceiling. Truth is, many working mothers don't want to travel, though travel can be key to advancing in your company hierarchy.

LEARN THE CULTURE OF YOUR COMPANY

Nancy heads a division of an international drug company. Before she was offered the job, she was thinking about starting a family. She had spent her twenties and thirties devoted to her career (long hours and lots of travel) and was now ready to give up the glamour of traveling. To learn how the company worked and what

---

would be expected of her, she questioned her prospective boss in a way to elicit helpful answers. "I know that there's a travel caveat," says Nancy. "The only thing that really matters in business is results. If you choose not to travel, and it impacts results, then you have a problem."

Travel Issues to Know First

- How does your boss feel about face time?
- Ask how much he or she travels.
- What are the boss's travel expectations for a person in the job?
- What does the boss expect you to do to be seen?
- Explain that if you travel, you lose at least one day. Find out whether there are alternative options to communication such as video- or teleconferencing.
- To find out what really goes on in any company, use your network. Check collateral sources such as your friends at competing companies or suppliers who have direct knowledge of the person who is interviewing you.

DON'T WANT TO GO?

The higher your position, the more you will be asked to travel. Linda is president of a television station whose parent company is across the country, and she travels to make presentations to the board. Chris is an attorney who often has to make negotiations and take important depositions in person, no matter where those people are.

Janet, though, elected not to travel in her job as a market analyst. "I didn't want to make those kinds of choices about whether a trip was important enough to take," she says. "My mother or mother-in-law would stay with my daughter, but I couldn't handle leaving all the time."

Whenever she was asked to travel, she tried to negotiate her way out of trips. "I'd suggest that someone else go in my place, and I began to delegate some of my responsibility to others so that they would be in a position to travel."

The result? Management perceived the willing travelers as more important to the company. Janet has been downsized twice recently and is now developing her own freelance consulting business.

The Best Travel Advice

Travel early in the job, make contacts with your clients and your boss, then make the decision to travel based on your relationships and knowledge of whether you really have to be there.

BANISH THE GUILT FROM YOUR MIND

One afternoon the car that was taking me to the airport for a one-night trip to Boston was in the driveway. I'd already said good-bye to the children and the baby-sitter, and as I put my bag in the trunk, my then-five-year-old daughter ran sobbing to the house, her pink T-shirt and shorts covered with mud. She thought I had left already, so she was running to her baby-sitter for comfort. I noticed an "Aha!" look in her eyes when she saw I was still there. She ran right to me and insisted I help her change into clean clothes. Of course I did it, even though I ran the risk of missing the plane. Those big eyes and loud cries do a lot to make you feel as though you should have no life of your own. And for as long as that offending pink T-shirt fit her, she'd always remind me, "Remember when this shirt got so dirty?" As if I could forget.

Ann is an account executive and often has to go to training sessions that can last more than a week. During one long trip, the worst nightmare came true: her daughter broke her leg. "My husband never called to tell me," she remembers. "He took care of the whole thing himself. He didn't want me to think about it, he said, but I know that he resents my being away and this was his way of showing me that if I were a good mother I would have been there. He needn't have worried. I was so guilty that I held my daughter for three days when I came home."

Dena's husband did call her when she was away on business to tell her that her toddler was in big trouble at school. Her habitual getting into fights and grabbing toys were causing the administrators to think about asking her to leave. "I was on a plane so fast," says Dena. "I already felt that her problems were my fault, that she needed me to help her channel her angry feelings, and it made me feel worse that this happened when I was away."

How to Take Some Control

Once you've made the decision to travel, don't look back. You feel guilty, but what good is it doing you? Nothing for your family life; nothing for the trip for which you need to be at top level. Instead of feeling bad, turn it around. Ask for certain criteria to make it easier for you to get home fast.

- No international travel.
- No traveling every week.
- No trips longer than five days.
- Must be home on weekends.
- Remember that no trip is so important that you can't leave in the middle of it.

Child Care Changes

Child care is quite different when you're out of town. It means for a baby-sitter longer hours and additional responsibilities, including more cooking and more decision making. That's why good child care is paramount.

- If your travel schedule is erratic, and you can't book a sitter in advance, use an agency that specializes in temporary care. Once you establish a relationship with the agency, you can request the same sitter again.
- Call in the relatives.
- Is there an older couple in your neighborhood or at your church or synagogue who might like to stay with your children when you're away?
- If you're away for only a night or two, arrange for your child to stay with a friend and then go to school together. Be sure to reciprocate.
- If you have a traveling husband, think about having live-in help so you don't have to scramble for child care every time you're both away.
- If you're a single mom and you incur great expenses because you always have to hire overnight sitters, talk to your boss about picking up a portion of the tab. Even though there may be no official policy, it doesn't hurt to ask.

IN THE END YOU HAVE TO RELY ON YOURSELF

Deborah learned this when she had to give a keynote address to a group in Alabama, and at the last minute still had no one to watch her three sons at home in New Jersey.

"My husband was out of the country, and neither my mother, best friend, nor regular sitter could stay with them. The only choice I had was to take them, have them wait for me in the hotel room while I gave the speech, and then go back to the airport and fly

---

home. But I had to make it sound positive. The night before I was to leave, I gathered them together and said, 'Boys, tomorrow you're going to have a great adventure. We're going to Alabama for the day.' It wasn't until long after they'd gone to bed—at 11:30 P.M.—that a sitter called back who could be there when they got home. We missed the great adventure, but I would decide to do it again."

How to Make Your House Hum While You're Away

- Have the family calendar/schedule in plain sight.
- Make a list on your computer that tells the person in charge (sitter, husband, relative) the whole schedule again. Print out two copies—one for each of you to carry. When you call home, you can review upcoming events.
- Have all important names and phone numbers next to activities.
- Arrange all the car pools in advance.
- Give your children a contingency plan in case things don't work out. Talk to them about what to do, whom to call, where to go if they're not picked up or if there's any emergency.
- Have a contingency plan for the person in charge.
- Find out if your child will need something special while you're away, and get it in advance.
- Get enough food in the house so that no one has to go shopping, especially for school lunches and snacks.
- Unless you have a cleaning person, don't even begin to assume the place will look halfway decent when you come home.
- Make sure someone knows how to do the laundry.
- Call home regularly.
- Don't fret if you'll be missing a school/kid event. Send someone in your place.

TIPS FOR HAVING VERY YOUNG CHILDREN

- Tell a preschool teacher when you're going to be away so he or she can be aware that your child may need some special attention.
- Too many phone calls may feel like too many good-byes for your children. You'll know best whether your children can handle it.

Nonbusiness Advice on
Having the Best Trip You Can

- Pack light. Do your best to have one carry-on bag. Believe me, they'll talk about you back at the office if you're the one with more bags than anybody else.
- Make sure you can manage your bags yourself. Surely, you already have one with wheels and a handle.
- If you're a frequent traveler, keep an extra toilet kit packed with everything you need, including makeup.
- Send your travel clothes to the cleaner as soon as you come home so you're ready to go the next time.
- Use your telephone credit card to make calls home. Sure, you hear you can make one call a day on the company, but with your own card you can feel free to talk as long as you like.
- Designate someone on the trip to know how you're all getting to and from the airport or train station, or where you're renting a car.
- Go to the hotel gym. If there's a fee to use it, put it on your own credit card.
- If you don't do gyms, take a walk near your hotel. You might as well learn something about the place you're visiting.
- Take a long bath. Remember, you're alone, and no one will hurry you out of the bathroom or ask for a snack.
- Always go back to your room alone at night. Legends are born on business trips.

- If you have a meeting scheduled with one man, arrange to see him in a public section of the hotel.
- Try to schedule something to discover the new city. You may want to come back with your family.
- Bring a little something home to the children. Don't shop too hard—find it at the airport.

READING ALOUD FROM ON THE ROAD

When her daughter was very young, Ruth would take on her trip the chapter book that they were in the middle of reading. Then she'd call every night and read a chapter to her daughter. Hillary Rodham Clinton had the same sort of plan. When she traveled, she'd leave an audiotape of herself reading children's stories so that Chelsea could hear her mom read before she went to bed at night.

Now Let's Get Out of Here!

There's a rallying cry for vacations. We're looking for a great escape from our highly organized lives. Oh, we might want tennis at ten, but it's quite different from using every minute to the best advantage until the school bus arrives at 7:42 A.M.

Don't put off taking the time to leave home and be with your family. No matter what appeals to you—a month in Europe or two weeks at the lake—this is your great bonding time, when you can have real conversations with your husband and children, make discoveries together, and take your family's pulse.

PLANNING THE GETAWAY
- Know the dates as far in advance as possible. This can help with hotel and transportation availability. You may be able to get better prices based on advance booking.
- If you're going to use some of your frequent flyer miles,

you have to arrange well in advance. The airlines do not make this easy.

- If you always return to the same place every year, make the next year's reservation when you're leaving.
- Have a budget. If you have a destination in mind, put a picture of it on your refrigerator, then make weekly contributions toward it.
- Get a travel agent. Do you really have the time to sit on hold waiting for the airlines or hotel, or make your way through the Internet trying to find great deals?
- Do some research on your destination so that you can plunge right in to your vacation. Have a couple of activities in mind (planned with your children).
- Take enough time off. Four-day weekend trips a few times a year might be nice for adults, but it's not great for families. Too much of your time is spent traveling, not enjoying.
- Travel with another family. Not only does it enhance your social life, but it makes things great for your kids when they have built-in friends.
- Don't cram your whole family into one hotel room. It's cheaper, but there are psychic trade-offs, with little chance for privacy, comfort, and relaxing. Think about a little cabin, an apartment, or a suite.
- Find out about house exchanges. A family from another city or country comes to stay at your house while you go to theirs.
- Take a baby-sitter with you. It works well when you're renting a house for a week or two and she has her own room or shares it with the children. Then you can have some free time during the day or in the evenings to do those things children find boring.
- Plan for your kids to have some downtime. Don't sightsee all day long, drag them to museums, or drive hundreds of miles. They hate it. Stop at a beach or a park. Plus they need to stop to eat a lot more than you might like.

Calling the Office

Remember, this is supposed to be a vacation. Don't walk around with your cell phone glued to your ear or your beeper stuck on your golf shorts. But if you must . . .

- Call once a day, period. Always make it at the same time, and don't do it in front of the family.
- Or just e-mail back to the office. Don't call, ever.
- Take a laptop so that you can communicate with the office. Answer your e-mail late at night or very early in the morning.

What About Those All-Inclusive Vacations?

Club Med had a great concept when it noticed that their customer base of carefree singles was growing older and wanted to go away with their children. The family club was born to offer a relaxing sociable time with plenty of activities for both parents and kids. Note that if you have preschoolers, there are weeks that they go free.

The best part, of course, is that you pay for it all before you go, and you don't have to plan anything.

There are lots of options available to you:

- Cottages at lakes with all kinds of family activities as well as more exotic destinations on the Islands or Mexico.
- Family camps and family cruises.
- Many hotel chains have picked up on this trend, too, and offer camps for the children. They also have bikes and small boats for the whole family to rent and nature trails to hike. Always see a picture of the hotel before you go. A water slide can sound a lot more fun in words; the picture tells more of the truth.
- Ski resorts have ski schools, plus activities that every child from preschooler to teenager can do after the lifts close.

- The Internet is filled with these kinds of choices, and a good travel agent will be able to tell you about the all-inclusive package appropriate for your family.

Have You Thought About a Camper?

Lots of families find this the best way to travel. They don't have to find a hotel or cottage in a busy beach-front community, for example, and it's like going away complete with your own living room.

- You can travel anywhere in the country at your own pace.
- Pull a car behind so that you'll be able to explore when you get to your destination.
- Look at a map before you go and figure out all the places you want to stop.
- Park it permanently in a wooded campground. Then go there on weekends. For some families it's as good as a two-week vacation.

AN INTERESTING ALTERNATIVE:
YOU STAY HOME AND YOUR KIDS GO AWAY

If you already have a teenager, you know that going away with you for a week at a time might not be at the top of her wish list. In fact, many parents talk about taking their "last family vacation." Instead, lots of kids will be happier going to visit a best friend's grandparents in Florida or California.

Alexa had an interesting solution. "Our daughter was beyond our family vacations," says Alexa, "so she went to Florida with a friend. We took the opportunity to take our younger son on vacation alone. This time we could design the vacation around something he likes. He likes music and art, and we heard about a town with summer stock and concerts, so we

---

went away as a threesome. He had our undivided attention, and he loved it."

Or maybe you might be happy with the kind of arrangement that Grace makes: "We take a big family vacation every summer," she says, "using the frequent flier miles that my husband earns all year with his business travel. But in the winter he takes the children away alone on a skiing trip. They are all superior skiers, and I can't even stand on them. It's wonderful because he's less restrictive than I am. He'll take them bobsledding or something I would never approve of. They always tell me about it afterward. I'm glad I don't have to be in the position to say no." When they're gone, Grace can work any kind of schedule she wants, either going in early mornings or staying late, then have dinner with colleagues.

Get Packing!

- Don't ever get into the habit of packing for your husband. It's very hard to break.
- Always make a list of what you have to pack.
- Remember that you are packing for yourself and your children. You have to remember everything for everybody, even if they're old enough to put things in the suitcase themselves. You're more likely to forget something for yourself than for your children—of course.
- When your children are small, and their clothes are little, pack all kids' things in one bag. Be sure to bring way more than you think you will need.
- Only bring diapers if you are going to a remote location where there won't be any. It's much better to buy them when you get there.
- Bring plenty of snacks to eat during traveling. Children of any age get cranky when they're hungry. Airline food is often strange, skimpy, and infrequent.

- Ask whether you can order fast-food meals for your children when you book your flights.
- Bring a small ball to play with so the kids can get outside and get some exercise. It's also a good way to meet other children.
- Do not forget the all-important stuffed animal.
- Bring a thermometer, children's Tylenol, antibacterial cream, and bandages.
- When your children are old enough (seven or eight), give them a list of what to pack. Have them lay out the things on their beds, then you check it and do the packing.
- If they are packing their own bags, check it yourself to make sure everything is in there.
- Starting at two years old, a child can bring his own little backpack filled with things he can do while traveling.
- When you arrive at the destination, unpack for your children right away. Show them where their clothes are, and designate a drawer for dirty clothes.
- Unless you're going to Antarctica, you can buy practically anything you forgot. Just call it a souvenir, and don't sweat it.

Have a great time. And don't forget your camera. But if you do, buy the whole family disposables.

▦ 8 ▦

Time for Time Off

Allow me to remind you how you met your husband.

It could have been on a blind date, at a bar, at a dance, at a party, even around the watercooler. It was somewhere that you were thinking about—even concentrating on—your social life.

These days, going out for a good time, parting with money that you know should go into your college tuition fund, and spending hours on the phone looking for a baby-sitter just because you want to go somewhere to entertain yourself can throw your guilt reactors into high gear and leave you feeling it's not even worth it.

Still, for many working mothers, a social life is what they miss most of all. We can all go nuts when we live the same trained-dog routine all the time. You need a social life— some rousing family time, some romantic time, and some let-off-steam girlfriend time—and you need to learn how to build it into your life.

"I'll go through the hassle of finding a sitter if I have to go out for my job. Otherwise, we don't have much of a social life."

—Carol, sales representative

The Easiest Way Is to Make Your Family the Basis of Your Social Life

One of the great benefits of having children is the wonderful friends that your family can make through them. You have a lot of reasons to bond: you like the same children, you want to be with your children, and your schedules are quite compatible. You know that it's difficult to drag (pardon me, encourage) your children to go out with another family when the children don't know each other.

Getting together with families of your children's friends creates a good time for your family and validates the choices of your children. As a parent you spend a lot of time helping your children make friends and showing them how to be a good friend. Sharing their friends with you is a great feeling.

FAMILY-FRIENDLY

Lorie's family developed a warm relationship with a family they met through soccer, and now they go away together for vacations. They've been to Disney World, to family resorts, and have rented condos at the beach. "It's not as though it was easy to find," says Lorie. "I looked for a relationship like this for thirteen years. I love that the children have another family—not just relatives—who care about them so much."

Encouraging Friendships

It's also possible, of course, to have a friendship with a family when you've met the mom or dad through work. Not as easy, when so many other people have to meet, but it has a greater possibility of working if the children are age-compatible.

Even when you really don't like one of the members of the couple, if one of their children is a great friend of one of yours then hold your nose and invite them. Just never invite the family alone. Make sure there's a family you enjoy also. Life is too short, and nonwork hours are too precious, to spend it with dreadful people.

What to Do with Another Family

- Keep it casual. No matter what your mother says, use paper plates. You're also giving your children a great message: it's the friends, the easygoing nature of the relationship, and the good feelings that are important.
- Crank up the energy and enthusiasm to get together. Just like exercise, the more you do it, the better you'll feel.
- When you get a notice from a play group, nursery school, sports league, or your elementary school that there's an event coming up, get on the phone immediately, call your child's best friend's parents, and make a date to get together right after the event. Then your two families stay after the picnic for a kickball game or to throw a football around. Or you go bowling, to a movie, or out for ice cream.
- Call on the spur of the moment for Sunday-night Chinese, either at your house or at a restaurant.
- Do easy Sunday brunches.
- Take weekend day trips for apple picking, hiking, visiting the zoo or a children's museum.
- Have frequent summer barbecues.

- *Always* let the other family bring part of the meal, or bring the whole meal, or cook it together.
- Take the kids to high-school, college, or professional sports games.
- Go to a play or kids' concert.
- Have a family tennis tournament or backyard baseball game.
- Meet at the community pool.
- Go shopping together: tag sales, antiquing, outlet centers, gourmet shops. Keep it fun, not your boring tedious errands.
- Include your own relatives, work friends who can bring their families, school family friends, and other friends on your guest list for a big casual gathering. The mix will work, and it's an easy way to return invitations.
- Remember that nobody is expecting you to entertain like Martha Stewart.

Sometimes You Just Have to Date Your Husband

You know what happens in a marriage. Your attention is diverted in eight million ways, and your husband is not at the top of the maintenance list. That's reserved for science projects, toilet training, and yard work. Your husband, you believe, is an adult who should be able to pull his own weight and meet his own needs, just as you think you should. You forget that nice give-and-take motion of a loving human relationship. But this is the guy you fell in love with, whose every word and gesture you adored. You got together as life partners, not as a maintenance team. Leap over the obstacles to make it work.

- Arrange a date even though going out on a Saturday night seems as complicated as planning a wedding.
- Get in social shape before you go out. Try going out with another couple or two at first, especially if you think your

social skills are a bit flabby. Translation: you can only talk
about work, your children, and the squirrels living in
your attic. Think about what's going on in the world,
what books you have read, trends you know about.
- Use your social evenings as a time to reconnect as adults.
- Remember the art of conversation.

NOT READY FOR DATE NIGHT

Susan and her husband both work very hard. For years
they *never* went out alone together. "I knew it was
about time we should go out alone, so we got a baby-
sitter, went out to a restaurant, ordered a drink, then
just sat and looked at each other. I kept thinking I
should reach over and wipe his chin or something. I
didn't know how to behave anymore. It was pathetic."
It happens to a lot of working moms.

TAKE TIME TO MAKE TIME

"We've established an unwavering bedtime for our children so that my husband and I always have a few minutes to talk before we go to sleep," says Alice. "We're
so exhausted ourselves that if we didn't start this early, it
wouldn't happen." At least when they go out, though,
they know who that person is across the table.

DOING DATE NIGHT
- Schedule it. (Sorry, but it's a fact of life.)
- Think of it as a date. You know, at least comb your hair
  and do something with your makeup. Changing your
  clothes would be nice.
- Don't spend the whole night talking about the kids and
  your jobs.

- A date night during the week (a quick dinner before you come home from the office) feels more spontaneous and thrilling than a Friday or Saturday night.
- Have a standing lunch date once a week.
- Make a date to play tennis or golf together, without the children.
- Go swimming together. It's a lot of fun—and sexy— when you don't have to give your kids bouncy rides.
- Find someone to stay for a night, and go away alone. Stay in a hotel. It does a lot to change the "roommate" relationship that many marriages of working couples succumb to. And, truth be told, it usually falls to the woman to keep the relationship on course.
- Get tickets in advance for a concert or theater. If a performer is coming to town that you and your husband remember from way back when, book it immediately.
- Have some imagination. Anybody can think of dinner and a movie. Do something weird you never do—go to a rock concert or a billiard hall or miniature golf course.
- When you have no kids at home—they're all at sleep-overs—go out!
- If you're going out with at least one other couple, pick a house where all the kids can stay, get two baby-sitters, and then go out. It makes it a great night for the kids, and they'll encourage you to go out rather than grumble about being left home.

CARPE DIEM

I've just had the amazing experience of having no children at home. They went away for two long (short?) weeks. (Is the glass half empty or half full?) The first night they were gone, my husband asked what I had gotten for dinner. I said, "Not only do I not have to make a proper meal, but we don't even have to eat dinner." We went to the movies and stopped for hot dogs. Hello, spontaneity. Grab it.

Single Moms Have a Life, Too

You are not doing your kids any favors by staying at home and feeling too guilty to go out because you think your children don't get enough parenting. Grown children of single mothers say they feel guilty because their mothers sacrificed for them all the time and didn't think of their own happiness. It's a big burden for a child to carry.

FIND YOUR OLD FRIENDS

Sandra had a lousy marriage. Her husband was sleeping with the next-door neighbor and eventually left her for a flight attendant. As you might imagine, their social life was lacking before they separated. The children didn't see any kind of family fun or parties, but after Sandra was divorced, she turned back to the friends she had known. She took her kids camping with her old friends and began the tradition of a New Year's Eve party at their home. "After we went camping the first time," says Sandra, "my eleven-year-old daughter told me, 'Mom, I never knew you had any friends. And they're really neat!' I'm glad I was able to show them some fun before they left home for college."

Back to Dating

Ah, dating. Open your eyes. You might not even know that the possibility is staring right at you.

BEING BOLD

Louise pursued a new relationship immediately. She was four months pregnant with her third child when her husband left her for an aerobics instructor.

"I was most comfortable in a coupled situation," she says, "so I called a male friend I'd known for years who had never married. I was hoping to work myself into his Saturday night date slot just so that I would have something to do besides work, take care of my other children, and be depressed. I never saw it as romance. Besides, I was pregnant! And when we fell in love, I had to be clandestine until the final divorce papers were filed." Today they're married.

Dating tips for single mothers:
- Keep your eyes open for relationships.
- Don't put your life on hold.
- Never get involved with a married man.
- Don't ask your children whether you should date.
- Think twice before you ask a man to sleep over. It sends a big message to your children.
- Don't try to turn a man into a substitute father.
- Don't discuss your dating life at work.
- Have your ex continue to share parenting duties such as picking kids up, going to events, and taking the children when you have a business trip. Remember, you're still working, and you still can't do it all alone.

The Girlfriend Connection

Friends are like a really good nap. When you were a little kid, they were a big part of your day, and you couldn't live without them. As you get older, you have more things going on in your life, and you reluctantly give up time with them.

As soon as you get to be an adult, you miss them, and once again can't live without them because they can refresh and rejuvenate you in only twenty minutes.

Still, friends, like naps, often fall to the bottom of our lists. You keep meaning to call or get together, but you don't have time.

But your pals are your lifeline to sanity. You know how men and women are said to be from different planets? Well, you need some time to regroup with your own species.

EVERYBODY MISSES FRIENDS

"I used to work with a group of women, and we became very close," says Jennifer. "We all moved on, but we kept getting together, until we all had children. Now we get together only once, maybe twice, a year. I miss them."

Dale says, "I still have one really good friend. We have to make time with each other because I can't deal with my life without her. We vent, and we can always pick up where we left off."

And Gerry laments, "I have more friendships with couples than with individual women, and I miss that. When you work it's hard. I have no time for tennis or lunch. The woman I'm closest to is a cousin who doesn't have children. I grab a phone call with her when I can."

"When our family moved from our old community," says Casey, "I knew I needed a mental health day, so I took a day off work and went to my old book group. All ten of the women sat around and let me vent. As good as a shrink, and certainly more fun."

The Best Way to Make Plans with a Friend

Most women will end a phone conversation with a friend with this kind of message: "Call me soon to let me know if I will call you to make that date that we say we really want to make but we're just not making." Bad idea.

Instead, say, "Get out your book, and let's make the appointment right now."

Come to a conclusion. Place the primary value on your own time that's convenient for you, your career commitments, and your family.

The greatest thing about women friends is that you can almost jump back into the conversation you last had. So your get-togethers don't have to be long.

- Breakfast. Meet right after you take your children to school. You might be a bit late to work.
- Saturday morning tennis game. Schedule it very early, before the children need you to take them to five thousand places.
- Schedule manicures or haircut appointments at the same time as a friend.
- Go to the gym together.
- Do an early morning walk together.
- Don't count on lunch. Too many obstacles such as unexpected meetings, trips, or business lunches can make you cancel and feel awful about it.
- Have a book group with your friends. You spend half the time talking about the book, the other half talking about different stuff.
- Make phone dates. You don't need to talk for an hour. Many times ten minutes is a great way to keep in touch.
- Use e-mail. It's fine, though not the greatest substitute, but it feels cozy to have a message that's not about a deadline for budget projections.
- If you go out of town on business to a city where you have a long-lost friend, call her before you go and schedule tea or drinks or dinner together.

- To get rid of your guilt, do trade-offs with your husband.
  He needs friends, too. You'll have to schedule those
  times in advance.

Having more of a life—outside of work, your children,
and your partner—can only enhance your spirit. What's
more, that's what gives you the vitality and renewed enthusiasm for all the roles you have to play. When you know
more people, who do all kinds of different work and share
with you their various interests, you'll be a more appealing
person, both to others and to yourself.

> *"HappyBirthdayMerryChristmas*
> *HappyHanukkahHaveaGreat*
> *FirstDayofSpring."*

▪ 9 ▪

Celebrations
Your Way

Do you get the feeling that birthday parties have gotten out of hand? How about this party for a two-year-old: a sit-down brunch for twenty children at a fancy restaurant with adult-size Mickey and Minnie, a storyteller, a princess, and a mime, complete with personalized tin crayon boxes filled to the brim with a year's supply. I'm not making this up. I was there.

What happened to cake, ice cream, Pin the Tail on the Donkey, modest party favors, and sending you on your way? All this is perfectly unnecessary.

You know what celebrations—birthdays and holidays—are about: happiness, togetherness, and a way to establish traditions and rituals that your children can remember all their lives.

That said, let me caution you that your role models for creating these perfect memories—Kodak and your mother— can be a bit skewed. Kodak, you already understand, is in the business of selling memories, and those people in the ads are actors. With your mother, it's a little more complicated. She probably didn't have a career the way you do and had a lot more time to conceptualize and carry out the plans.

What's more, there was a time when there were specific rules for the way things were done. We don't live like that now. We're much freer to invent and establish our own ways to celebrate.

You won't do it exactly as your mother did. And you can't feel bad about it. Take on the responsibilities of the holiday celebrations and do it in your own style.

Birthdays Actually Are National Holidays

Doing birthday parties does not have to be a problem. Just make sure you start off from Birthday One with the right attitude. If you begin to outdo yourself from the beginning, you're going to have to continue to outdo your own excesses year after year. You love your children, to be sure, but do you have time for all this outdoing? Honestly, all a little kid needs is a couple of hours with friends and family and a rousing rendition of Happy Birthday.

IT'S WHOSE PARTY?

You get into trouble when you think that your child's party has to be so different from that of every other child. That's not what young children want. "I look at these other parties, and I often feel that I'm not doing it well," says Ruth. "I wonder if I'm shortchanging my daughter by not spending enough time at it. But I know that any of it will suck up as much time and energy as you give to it. And I don't have it to part with."

Kids want the same party everyone else has. Every time my children come home from a party, they want one just like it. Until they go to the next party.

The First Rule of Convenience: Have It Out

One-year-olds can have a small party at home. But starting at age two, you'll do better not to do it yourself. One of the greatest new businesses for you is the birthday party business.

EASY PARTIES

"I know I couldn't think of a way to amuse the children and do the whole party," says marketing consultant Beth. "So I always find a place to have it. It costs more, but I work, and I have money to pay for it."

Kate and her friends all settled on the same place for parties. "We tried a lot of different places, but they can be exhausting for the parents. They're too noisy or crowded, but when one of us had a pool party at our community indoor pool, that was it. The lifeguards take the kids into the water, and it's like a spa day for all the moms. We sit on the sidelines and drink wine and have a great time. We've agreed to have parties for all our kids there."

WHY YOU HAVE A PARTY SOMEWHERE ELSE
- You don't have to clean your house before the party.
- You don't have to clean your house after the party.
- You don't have to watch all the children yourself, and you don't have to ask other parents to stay.
- You don't have to think of entertainment.
- You don't have to go through the hassle of finding a clown or magician.
- You just show up.
- All you have to bring is the cake.
- You don't have pizza stuck to your living-room sofa.

WHERE TO HAVE IT

- A movie theater (ages five and up). Find one with a party room so that you can have pizza and cake after the movie. Some theaters have Saturday afternoon birthday specials with lucky-number drawings, special snacks, and favors for the children.
- An indoor playspace (ages two–eight). These facilities also have party rooms. Some let the children loose for an hour to play, some have supervised activities.
- Local Y (ages three and up). You can have soccer parties, swimming parties, basketball parties, gymnastics parties. Check to see what your Y offers.
- Fast-food restaurants (ages two–six). Check those which have outdoor climbers.
- Kid-size arcades (ages five–eight). They also have party rooms and special treats for birthday kids.
- Skating rink (ages six and up). Ice or roller skates.
- Haircutting salons (ages five–seven) often have birthday parties for girls.
- Children's theaters (ages five and up).
- Children's museums (ages five–eight).
- Theme restaurants (ages six and up).
- Craft facilities (ages four and up). Plaster painting, ceramic painting, spin art.
- Bowling alley with bumper bowling (ages five and up).
- Professional, high-school, or college sports event (ages seven and up).
- Preschools and music or dance schools often do birthday parties on weekends when the schools are closed.
- You can also rent large spaces (at schools, community centers, churches) and have your own entertainment. Bring in a clown, a magician, a puppeteer, a nature presenter, performers who put on plays or have kids do their own, face painters, balloon twisters, or artists who create and supervise projects.
- Ask friends, read ads, get recommendations to find the best people. Just know that the best ones, of course, are booked far in advance.

WHO'S COMING?

Keep your guest list near your family calendar so that when moms call to RSVP, anyone in the house can check off the names.

The Party Difference Between
Little Children and Big Children

LITTLE: FROM ONE TO FIVE

The party rules—written by some party psychologist, I suppose—say that you should have the same number of children as your child's age, plus one. It's not a bad idea. How many good friends does a two-year-old have anyway?

Still, with children in so many groups and classes, they can get invited to many parties. You can end up with a large group. But a one- or two-year-old is not offended by not being invited. Only the parent is.

- If you choose to do an at-home party, keep it simple. Your child is too small—and so is the party—to have clowns and magicians. Besides, most one- and two-year-olds are scared to death of people in costumes.
- For these little ones, have them play in the yard, the playroom, or your child's room, and give them a little coloring activity and cake. That's really what they want. Ask the other parents to stay.
- When you have a three-year-old, you can start having parties at places other than your home.
- Hire a babysitter or two to help.
- You might need parents to stay.
- Have parents transport their children to the party place. Many parents of young children feel uncomfortable putting their children into the cars of others.

BIG: SIX AND UP

The window of opportunity for clown parties is quite short. Three-year-olds may be terrified, but seven-year-olds will be bored out of their minds and forever insulted that anyone thinks they would still like to see a clown. Your party needs to get a bit more grownup. The sports and crafts parties work. And you have now entered the world of the sleep-over.

For a working mother, the sleep-over is one of the easiest parties to give. It takes minimal time, planning, even presence on your part. Be home, of course, but they don't want to see you much.

How to live through a sleep-over party:

- Five is about the most you can handle.
- Don't have them come too early or stay too late. Have them get to your house at six P.M. and leave by eleven A.M., at the latest.
- Rent plenty of videos.
- Order pizza. Has your child ever been to a birthday party that didn't have pizza?
- Have tons of snacks. Tell your child what all the snacks are and exactly where they are in the kitchen so that you can be as far removed as possible.
- You can combine it with an outside activity first: meet at a movie, a play, swimming pool, skating rink, arcade, or miniature golf course, bowling alley, or a crafts place, and then go to your home.
- Unless they're making too much noise and keeping a younger child up, don't worry too much about falling asleep. (Better yet, send the younger children to Grandma's.)
- Have a great breakfast. Make chocolate-chip pancakes or waffles or French toast or muffins.

Sending Cupcakes to School

This goes on for many years.

- Get them at the supermarket. They have tons of frosting on them and come in plastic boxes that keep them separate so they won't be totally destroyed on the school bus. Well, they may, but it won't be your fault.
- Brownies (get a mix!) or Rice Krispie treats are both extremely easy to make.
- Make treats in disposable aluminum pans that you never want to see again. Pack in a big shopping bag for your children to carry to school.

Shopping for Birthday Presents and Party Favors

You will not endear yourself to any mother if you give the latest I-have-to-have-it junky toy, and if you distribute a party bag filled with candy and a few awful trinkets that no one even cares about getting. If you know the mother well enough to ask what present the child wants, do, or follow these guidelines:

BIRTHDAY PRESENTS
- **For little ones:** easy puzzles, picture books, games, stuffed animals; toddlers like big trucks, ride-on toys, pull toys, art supplies.
- **For preschoolers:** simple art kits, picture books, games, cars and trucks, big-block sets, self-contained playsets with dishes, farms, or houses, simple dress-up items like capes or hats.
- **For young schoolchildren (kindergarten–second grade):** books (maybe a kids' poetry anthology or folk tales that parents can read aloud), kid versions of big-kid games like Monopoly, simple kits of building blocks, art kits (clay or painting or easy bead-stringing).
- **For older schoolchildren (third–fifth grades):** a few paperbacks based on their reading level, crafts kits (jew-

elry, lamps, picture frames, for example), games, more difficult block-building sets, science kits, magic kits, stationery sets.
- Shop at a store that does gift-wrapping and sells cards, too.
- No one wants clothes.

TAKE TIME TO MAKE TIME

Have a little stockpile of gifts so that you don't have to find the time to shop for every party. And if your child isn't invited to as many parties as you anticipated, it means less shopping for you at Christmas or Hanukkah.

FILLING THE UBIQUITOUS PARTY BAG
- For any age, keep the candy to a bare minimum—or forget it altogether.
- It's faster and easier to shop for the same decent inexpensive gift for everybody. Depending on the age, get little stuffed animals, key chains, lots of pencils, a little decorated box, trial-size shampoos and creams, a box of crayons or markers, a little three-dimensional puzzle, sports cards, discount coupon for a local restaurant or movie theater.
- Find a shop that makes party favors you can pick up: mugs filled with pencils, baskets with soaps, personalized team caps.
- Have the children make their own favors at the party: easy necklaces, friendship bracelets, painted boxes, ceramics, picture frames (with instant pictures you take at the party), painted T-shirts or aprons, painted rocks for bookends, paperback books.
- If you're giving the party at an outside place, they can often help with ideas for good party favors.

Here Come the Holidays

Thanksgiving, Christmas, Easter, Rosh Hashanah, Passover, and Kwanza come once a year. Every single year. So decide once how you want to do it, and figure out the most efficient way to plan it.

Know the way you want to celebrate:
- Decide the order of importance: family time, food, friends, rituals, memories, traditions, decorations, peace, active partying. Then concentrate your holiday efforts according to your priorities.
- Don't try to do everything every year.
- When you've determined the way you want to celebrate, let your extended family know.

OUR OWN HOLIDAYS

"My husband and I are so busy," says Carla, "that we decided to set our own Christmas traditions. We told our parents that we'll have a big family dinner on the twenty-fourth, then it's our little family together on the twenty-fifth. They understand."

"I was performing up to everyone else's expectations and going crazy," says Frances, who's an assistant to the president of a large company. "I have so many business obligations at that time of the year. I wanted to see my friends and my family for Christmas, too, but we've decided to alternate years. One year we'll have a nighttime party for friends, the next year have a brunch for our relatives."

How to Have Your Family Over for the Holidays

Holidays are one time you really should listen to your mother and not use the paper plates.

This is when you drag out the wedding presents.

Your house should be clean.

Your table should be set with a real tablecloth.

You'll send the message that holidays are special—times to stop what you're doing in your day-to-day crazy life and notice the people around you.

PLANNING IT

- Invite everyone early so they know you're the one who's doing the holiday.
- Don't take on all the cooking yourself. Ask relatives to bring dishes, have the whole thing catered, or order some of it.
- Decide what serving platters you need. Either make a list of which ones you're using and what food goes on them or lay them out with little notes on them.
- Assess your supplies. Make sure you have enough glasses, napkins, and chairs, and check that the big red wine stain on your tablecloth is gone.

ENTERTAINING THE OLD-FASHIONED WAY

- Set the table as far in advance as possible.
- Get help, especially for dishwashing. You don't really want all your relatives in the kitchen washing the dishes, do you? Ask a baby-sitter if she wants to help (she can also entertain the kids when the adults are sitting at the table talking) or call a household-help agency in your area.
- Don't serve anything that has to be prepared at the last minute.

TAKE THANKSGIVING, FOR EXAMPLE

Get it down to a science.

Two Weeks in Advance
- Plan the menu.
- Call everybody who's reliable to see what they can bring.

- Order some dishes, the appetizers, or desserts from a caterer.
- Line up household help.
- Rent chairs, china, wine glasses, whatever you need.
- Order wine to be delivered.

Saturday Before
- Open a cookbook to find out what to make and then what you need to buy.
- Make out the shopping list for shopping on Sunday.

Sunday
- Get the groceries.
- Order a fresh turkey from the supermarket.

Tuesday Night
- Make stuffing.
- Make one dessert.

Wednesday Night
- Set the table.
- Put out the platters, bowls, serving pieces.

Thursday Morning
- Get up at the crack of dawn to stuff the turkey.
- Pick up any dishes you've had prepared by a caterer or a local food shop.

Thursday Afternoon
- The family arrives with the dishes they've made.
- They sit down to eat.
- Look relaxed.

WANT TO CELEBRATE BUT YOU HAVE NO RELATIVES TO INVITE?

With the nature of our career moves, we often live far from home. Our families are spread around, and if a big family holiday comes at a time during the week when it's too complicated to travel, we end up feeling sad and bereft.

It's up to you, then, to take charge and make the holiday happen with friends. Your church or synagogue will be delighted to match you up with other families in your same situation. Or they probably even have holiday celebrations at your place of worship. You can create holiday traditions with your friends.

Invite friends to join you. Keep it simple and collaborative. You're creating the traditions. No one is comparing you to your mother, your grandmother, or your great-aunt. The way you do it is the right way to do it.

For Those Who Must Find Time to Decorate the House

If your parents always had an elaborate Christmas tree with a reconstruction of their hometown in miniature underneath, spend about two minutes feeling bad you're not doing it. Then accept that you'll always be getting your tree and a wreath or two at the last minute. Your children still understand the meaning of Christmas.

- Try to take off a week at the holidays to get ready. Work extra hard the week before and the week after.
- Have a florist come in and decorate your house with greens.
- Pick up pots of cyclamen, a flowering plant that lasts for months, so you won't have to hurry to throw out poinsettias after the holidays.

- Buy a gingerbread house instead of making one.
- Use the decorations your children make at day care and preschool.
- Get the help of your children, no matter what their ages.
- Take it slow. Instead of decorating your whole tree at once, make an advent tree, and put a new bulb or decoration on every day.

Shop, But Not Till You Drop

- Forget the last-minute shopping. Nobody wants a gift from the corner drugstore or something picked up in desperation at the mall.
- Shop during your vacations when you are in a shopping mood and browsing for souvenirs.
- Get on the mailing lists for catalogs. Take a couple of nights to go through them, place your orders, and then you're done.
- Shop when you're out of town on a business trip and have a few minutes to yourself.
- Shop during the summer, especially in July, when the stores aren't crowded. If you think you can't get in the holiday mood, just close your eyes and imagine huge mobs of people shoving toward frazzled sales help. It works.
- Shop on the Internet. Search by category or specific retailers.
- Keep a list of things that you want and that you have heard others in your family want.
- Buy something when you see it. Don't go back for it.
- Have a few extra generic gifts (books, scarves, household decorations, kitchen gadgets) that you can give to somebody you didn't expect who shows up with something for you.
- Don't even consider spending hours in the kitchen craft-

ing gifts of gourmet chutneys, vinegars, or sauces and decorating them spectacularly. Let somebody give that to you.

No matter what holidays you celebrate, just be sure to celebrate them. Keep the joy, the tradition, the significance alive. Don't give your children the message that holidays are a hassle for you, that they're something you'd rather not do. It's a time to appreciate your family, your roots, and your future.

▦ 10 ▦

Finding the
Time to Raise
the Right Kind
of Child

When you really think about it, being organized enough to straighten up your living room, get your children out of the house in the morning, and pick them up at day care isn't that hard. You need a pencil, a piece of paper, a watch, a calendar, and a bit of logic.

What's hard is that other part of being a mother: turning your innocent, guileless, perfect baby into an adult who's caring, compassionate, sensible, and responsible.

The difficulty of raising a moral child is a hotly debated topic, especially as some in our society continue to attribute the downfall of civilization and the rise of an MTV culture of smart-mouthed, belligerent, materialistic children to a legion of working mothers' total lack of moral leadership.

We feel terribly guilty that we're not around all the time to guide our children through the minefield of life. We work hard, we work late, and we're distracted. Outside influences are more pervasive and threatening. As much as we want to think of nothing but our children when we're home, thoughts of impending deadlines or sagging bottom lines creep into our thoughts. We fear that because we're not around enough we'll miss the seven warning signals of everything.

Your children will be confronted with choices—about places to go, people to go with, how much money to spend, and what to do when you get there. You want to be sure that the value system they take with them is yours and is solid. You might not have a lot of hours to teach it, but you have to make the best use of the moments you capture.

First, Pay Attention to What You Say and How You Say It

From the beginning, your children hold you in the highest regard and listen to your instructions no matter how much you're away from home. (That changes as the years go on, not because your opinions are less valid, only because your children are more independent.)

- Be conscious of the way you interact with your husband, your mother, your sister, the dry cleaner, and the baby-sitter. The way that you talk to others shows your children the kind of respect that you believe people deserve.
- Take time to talk to your children about being good people. Point out examples.

The Smallest Children Can Learn the Biggest Lessons

Start on the changing table. By the time your child goes to day care, he or she will have to know these lessons quite well.

- Your actions can make other people happy.

- When people are sad, help them feel better.
- Share.
- Decide in advance to do something nice for another person.
- All people are equal.

How to Know What's Going on with Your Children

You have to take the time, and you need to know how to approach them.

LISTEN

- Try to encourage a life of dialogue so that when you get a call from your child at the office, you can hear what's behind the voice.
- Talk to your nanny, baby-sitter, or whoever is spending the day with your child. You really have to rely a lot on others to know what is going on.
- If you're in the front seat of a car, and kids are in the back seat, after a while they don't acknowledge that you're there, and you hear all kinds of wonderful stuff.

NOT HARD OF HEARING

Erica: "My daughter and I have a relationship I would have died for with my mother. When she was in elementary school, she asked questions about God and said, 'If you're not truthful, I'll get the information somewhere else.' I heard that loud and clear."

Bonnie: "It's difficult to get things out of my third-grade son. Sometimes I get a hint when I overhear him on the phone talking to a friend or when he tells me he hates his teacher or that he got into trouble but it was really someone else's fault. I never let these go by. When I put him to bed, I'll lie down with him and talk. Anything is better than going to sleep. It's relaxing,

---

and it's easy to start a conversation. He'll tell me about a problem, and I'll give him a choice of things he could do to solve it, then I tell him to let me know if he needs help."

CAPTURE MOMENTS

Make the best use of the time you have together.

- Find run-of-the-mill, unscheduled time to connect.
- Don't spend a Saturday driving silently back and forth to activities or playdates.
- Don't let them sit for hours in front of the television or computer when you're home.
- Stop together at night and comment on the beautiful sunset. Or take a moment in the morning to appreciate the peace together.
- If you have to go to the office on a Saturday, don't get a sitter, take your child and talk on the way.
- Take the time before bed to lie down and talk in the dark. Day-care workers often talk about how tired the children of working mothers are. Big deal. They'll take a longer nap.
- Have the kids hang out in the kitchen with you when you're getting dinner ready.

WATCH FOR A MOMENT

Ruth: "As much as I dislike television, I'll watch *Fresh Prince* and *Family Matters* with my daughter. Those shows can get you into conversations about issues, and we'll talk about it right then."

GET TO KNOW THEIR FRIENDS

- Don't let your sitter be the only adult who has contact with your children's friends.
- When your child has a playdate at your house on the weekend, take time to talk to his or her friend. Eat lunch or dinner with them and have a conversation. Notice manners, language, how the kids interact.
- See who your child has chosen to bring home.

FRIENDS NEED TO KNOW WHERE YOUR CHILD IS COMING FROM

Beth: "I know I overcompensate and take too much on. I like to have kids over if there's an opportunity. Last Halloween I had my daughter invite seven girls over for pizza before they went trick-or-treating. This is her house, and I want her to feel free to have friends here—when I'm home. I want to know who she hangs out with, and I want them to know me."

PLAN FAMILY ACTIVITIES

Everyone needs to decompress after a hard week during the weekend. It doesn't always have to be alone in a bathtub.

- Try decompressing with the family.
- Don't make it a required ritual; you don't want them to feel guilty if they accept an invitation with a friend.
- Set up a puzzle on the dining-room table, have a cooking project, go on a hike, have a backyard game. Do something that gives the children a comfortable time to talk if they feel like it.

GIVE YOUR CHILDREN THE OPPORTUNITY TO TALK TO SOMEONE ELSE

- Let your children get close to other adults whom you respect.
- A relationship with an extended family member, or a friend you consider as close as family, gives them another person to turn to, a person who will then tell you what's going on.

ASK THEM QUESTIONS TO LEARN WHAT THEY THINK

You think you know how your child would react to a situation?

- When you hear a story on the news that might be a catalyst for conversation, or your child tells you something about a friend, ask how your child feels, and then talk about it.
- Don't pry; make it a conversation. Piercing questions slam the door shut.
- If your child asks you how to handle a situation, give the question back to her. Then at least you know where to begin the discussion.

ROLE-PLAYING

Regina: "We heard about a little boy on the street who got into a car with a stranger. Even though I had told my son a million times not to do it, now I could ask him what he thought could happen, and he could really think of the consequences."

CHECK YOUR CHILDREN'S MORAL VITAL SIGNS.

- Ask them what they want to be when they grow up.
- Ask them who they admire.
- After you've talked about a heavy subject, bring it up again in a reasonable amount of time (just a day or two for a toddler or preschooler and a week later for a

school-age child) and find out how things are going. No kid wants you breathing down his neck, but he does want you to check in.

- Let children know that they can always talk to you when there's a problem.
- Be available to them.
- If you need it, have a beeper.
- Use e-mail from your office to initiate a conversation with your school-age children and to communicate about any concerns that might come up when you're on the road.

TAKE A POSITION AND HAVE A STRATEGY BEFORE YOU TALK ABOUT SEX AND DRUGS

- Bring it up when your child is ready to talk about it, not when you have time between meetings.
- Make sure the opportunity doesn't pass you by. My children's elementary school principal tells the story of a fifth-grade girl who informed the hygiene teacher that she had had her period for four months and was afraid to let her mother know.
- At the school's curriculum night find out when the subject will be introduced that year (it starts with a self-esteem class in kindergarten) and be prepared for questions.
- No, you do not have to be perfectly honest about your past.

CONFRONT PROBLEMS WHEN THEY COME UP

As soon as you hear something has happened, talk about it. But first take a deep breath. If there's a conflict, find out all sides of the story. Your child is never all wrong and never all right.

- Be sympathetic.
- Come home early from the office if you can. It's difficult for a child to sit waiting and worrying about what you think and what your reaction might be.
- Follow through. Deal with the school or the other child's

parents, depending on the problem. It shows your child that work isn't so important that you can't direct your activities to helping your child.

SET YOUR STANDARDS

Beth: "My eleven-year-old daughter loves to argue with me. I've taken privileges from her, which works for a bit. Things didn't change until I told her to stop apologizing to me. Her apologies seemed empty and noncommittal. I said, 'Don't apologize. Show me that you mean what you say.' It took her a while to understand that."

Roseann: "I'm very tough about table manners and saying please and thank you as though you mean it. My kids hate it, but I don't care. I'm raising them to live in our society, and they have to know what the standards are.

"When I go to a business lunch, and I see someone who doesn't know how to hold a fork or eats with his mouth open, all I can think is, 'Didn't he have a mother?' People notice manners. Every time my children go to someone's house, the parents always tell me how well-mannered my children are."

Disciplining When You're Not There to Carry It Through

- First, learn to say no. All children need limits. You hear it all the time, but look at all the kids doing whatever they want.
- Know what your limits are.
- Have rules about television watching, time on the computer, telephone calls, table manners, curfews, how one talks to an adult, writing thank-you notes, calling grandparents, eating vegetables, doing chores, taking phone messages, bedtimes, baths and showers, holding doors open for others, shaking hands, giving your seat to an

older person on the bus, swearing, whining, and throwing temper tantrums.

- Don't expect that they will ever thank you for setting limits. But letting them know what is expected of them helps them to define their moral choices.
- When your children do something wrong, when they make you angry or don't follow the rules, punish them. They're going to feel bad. But that's okay. You should feel bad when you do something wrong.
- Give time-outs judiciously, even to yourself. Go into your own room and cool down.
- Authorize your sitter to give time-outs.
- Taking away privileges is still the most effective punishment. You can be sure that takes effect, especially if you take something tangible.

TAKE TIME TO MAKE TIME

Let your relationship with your children evolve naturally. They need to develop into the people they will be. We're all born with a personality, and we change and grow, but that basic person is who we are. You can shape your child and direct his focus, but you have a moral responsibility to support the individual.

Raising children is always a surprise. That's the beauty and the beast of it. You're constantly called on to adapt. "I couldn't have imagined how my boys would change," says Christine. "They are completely different people today from the toddlers and preschoolers they were five years ago. I had to give up all my preconceived notions about what it would be like to have children. I let it flow. I listen to them and encourage them to share their experiences. I had to accept that I have no control except to guide them."

HOW DO YOU SPEND?

When Andrea's son went to every friend's house, they had Nintendo 64. Starting in September, the Christmas commercials pervaded their home. Her son begged for it. "I thought I was being vigilant," says Andrea, "but I started to feel sorry for him for not having it. I bought it even though it wasn't Christmas or his birthday. I said to myself, 'What's wrong with you, Andrea? This is just from guilt.' It's a substitute for not being there."

Kids and Your Dual Income

"Spoiled" and "materialistic" are two words you do not want to hear when anyone describes your children. But could it happen to you?

Children can be lulled into thinking that your dual-income lifestyle allows for reckless spending on vacations, sneakers, computers, designer clothes, and new cars.

You might be giving them money because you feel guilty that you're not giving them time. They might get an allowance and still you'll throw them a few bucks when they want to buy something.

Someone has to tell them that people work hard for money.

Money has the power to send you out of the house every day, to make you argue, make you happy, and make you frantic. Of course children can think it's the most important thing in the world.

You need to teach your children how to earn it, spend it, save it, and, most important, how to put it in perspective.

TELL YOUR CHILDREN WHAT MONEY MEANS

My daughter and I have a little ritual some evenings. After dinner, we'll put on our jammies and sit on my bed together and read. One night when she was six or so, I was reading the paper, and she asked me what I was reading. I told her about a family that could afford only to share one box of macaroni and cheese between four people and to have only one light at a time on in the house.

She had just eaten almost a whole box of macaroni and cheese for dinner herself and was planning on taking the rest for her lunch the next day. She looked at me wide-eyed. I realized that she was ready to learn the value of a dollar. I started talking to her more and more about how much it costs to maintain a household. My children both thought that electricity was free and that you didn't have to put any money into the cash machine, you just took it out.

"My children have a very abundant life," explains Deborah, who grew up poor in New York's East Harlem. "I expose them to a variety of people who don't live as well—even in our own family. In my business, I employ people who have a range of salaries, and I explain to my children what minimum wage is and how people budget for their needs based on different incomes."

Your children have a lot of outside influences, but the most important influence comes from you. "We are not rich," says Amy, "but my son always tells me he's going to be rich. I try to impress on him that it doesn't come from miracles, and I tell him that if he wants to make a lot of money, he better study very hard."

How about grandparents, who are always ready to buy for your children? "My daughter has four sets of grandparents," says Shawn, "and they're very hard to control. I think they spoil my daughter; my mother buys her way too much. I tell them how I feel about it, but they tell me this is the way grandparents are."

You have to give them some room, but also give them some guidelines. They should know if you don't approve of purchases such as violent toys or certain kinds of clothing.

Put Your Children on the Right Path

Just because you have the money doesn't mean you have to buy them every single thing they ask for. Teach them to have priorities. And have them yourself.

Ask yourself:

- Do I actually have the time to run all over the place looking for certain brands and labels and toys of the moment?
- Am I giving my child the message that buying more stuff makes me happy?
- Would I buy my child another pair of brand-new sneakers just to match the other kids in the class?
- Do I want to be the final arbiter on how my child's allowance or birthday checks from relatives are spent?
- Am I giving any of my income to charities—and does my child know it?
- Do I spend way too much on my children and neglect myself?
- Am I telling my children that they can wait to have things like their own televisions, telephones, and computers?
- Can I substitute time for money and feel comfortable about it?

TEACH THEM HOW TO SHOP

- Teach them the difference between needs and wants. Make a list of three needs and three wants before you go shopping. Needs always come before wants.
- Have an idea of what things cost before you go shopping,

and set a spending limit.
- Let your child know when the limit is spent—that's it.
- Take your children grocery shopping.

    This is one of the first places they learn about money. A one-year-old can hand the money to the cashier. A five-year-old can help clip coupons. A ten-year-old can help decide which products are most economical.

TEACH THEM HOW TO SPEND
- Give them a weekly allowance.

    Allowances start when you think your child needs money to spend—usually around nine, certainly by twelve. Many parents give a dollar per year of age. Theirs, not yours.

    Give them enough money so that they'll be able to buy what they want and save some for special things.

    Don't tie the allowance to chores. This is not a salary. Also, when you get a raise, give your child a raise.

- Tell your child how the allowance is to be used.

    It's for all the stuff they want to buy that's beyond the necessities that you provide. It's for the movies they want to see with friends, and the extra popcorn.

- Don't bail your kids out.

    If they buy something they don't like or that breaks, don't offer to replace it. That's a life lesson.

- Starting with babies, don't buy your children a present every time you go out together. If you're going to a museum, that's enough. No rule says you have to stop in the gift shop before you leave.

- Set goals for saving.

    Going on vacation? Your child can buy her own souvenirs.

How to Handle the Holidays

- Make a wish list.

    Write it all out, unedited. Then go over it with your child, and have him decide what he could live without.

- Have the same budget for each child.

    An eight-year-old is savvy enough to understand the budget concept, and many of them seem to know how much everything costs. Tell a child, for example, that the budget is $200. Let your child know that it can be one big thing or twenty little things.

- Make an offer to share the cost with grandparents or aunts and uncles if your child wants something over the budgetary limit.

The Last Word on Morals: Responsibility

"It's not my job."

   "Nobody ever told me to do that."

   "It's not my fault."

   "I couldn't help it."

   "It's too hard to do."

Everybody says they're disgusted with these whiny excuses, but we continue to hear them. You can take a stand to help them stop. All you have to do is tell your children three things:

   1. Everything you do has an effect on somebody.

   2. Take responsibility for the choices you make.

   3. Admit your mistakes and go on.

Oh, I almost forgot:

   4. Be good to your parents in their old age. They love
      you.

▪ 11 ▪

The Working Mother Goes to Work

Down at the office, nobody has the faintest idea you're up with a colicky baby every night, that your daughter learned to swim, or that on weekends you like nothing better than a rousing game of backyard kickball. For a long time, nobody cared either. You had to keep it to yourself, revealing to no one that inside your proper suit and heels was a mom in a T-shirt and shorts.

Life has changed in corporate America. Women fill in the blanks on many organizational charts—about half the positions in the workforce. Although women still hold less than five percent of the senior management positions in the big corporations, we occupy a big enough position in the workforce that we've been able to effect change.

A lot of the change has come because now daddies want to be part of their children's lives, to have a greater participatory role than their own fathers did, and they've seen, too, that the rewards of work are not quite what they imagined they would be. And as a generation of older male managers has observed their own daughters and daughters-in-law struggle and juggle with their children, they've let some decent policies creep into their human resources departments.

Still, standards continue to be different for women—particularly for mothers—than they are for men. Recognize the truth, live with it, work to change it, help other working mothers deal with it as you slog through the realities of the workforce.

When You're About to Become a Working Mother

You have a lot on your mind, not the least of which are the responsibilities of your particular job. Your relationship to your job is about to change forever.

First, know your company's human resource policies:

- See whether your company is eligible to participate in the Family and Medical Leave Act of 1993. This entitles you to take a twelve-week unpaid leave after you give birth or adopt a child, and your employer must hold your job or a similar one as well as continue to pay your benefits.
- Can you structure a flexible schedule?
  Be sure you really want it because you'll probably take yourself off the fast track leading to a line-management position. Have an idea of where you want to go in your career.

WHAT HAPPENS IN A SHORTER WEEK?

When you do structure a three- or four-day workweek, "you're often going to have to do just as much work although it might be from home," says Bonnie, a human resources director who pressed her company until they agreed to offer flexible schedules.

> "It's hard to be a manager when you work three days a week," says Carol, a banking executive. "Projects take longer, and my patience is strained when I'm waiting for things to get accomplished."

- Find out whether there is a handbook—or work to create one if you don't have a human resources department—that details maternity leaves, medical insurance coverage, a dependent-care assistance plan, plus leaves to care for sick or aging family members.

When to Tell Them the Baby's Coming

- Keep it a secret as long as you can, advise most moms.
- Wait until the fourth month, until you're past the most likely time for problems such as miscarriages and those picked up by amniocentesis. Let them wonder and whisper about how fat you're getting.
- Know how long you'll be out for maternity leave. Be honest with your employer. Have your child-care arrangements in place or under serious consideration.
- When you tell your boss, make the decision together about how and when you will tell others in the office.

If there's a big project or meeting coming up in which you have a lot of responsibility, you may decide to postpone spreading the news until the crunch is over.

- If you're a manager, have a succession plan so that your people know who is responsible when you are not around. Ensure that someone could step in to take your position.
- Take yourself out of a lot of the meetings and day-to-day decision making before you leave so that people will know how to work without relying on you. Stay involved in an advisory capacity.

- Agree on the terms for coming back to work and working from home.

YES, I AM NOT AVAILABLE

Nancy told her supervisor that she would be out for three months, and together they agreed that when she came back, she would work six-hour days for the first two months. "He asked whether I would do some work from home during my leave, and I said I would, toward the end," she recalls. "There was a crisis in my department during the leave, and they asked me to come in to the office. I didn't really want to, but I asked whether I could come in wearing jeans and to have a private spot—not my regular office—where I could work. It was fine, and it was the only time they asked me to come in."

- When someone says to you, "Surely you're not really coming back to work after you have that baby, are you?" answer, "Surely you're not asking any other pregnant woman that question. It's illegal."
- Continue to do the best work you can during your pregnancy. Your hormones are powerful chemicals that can make you emotional, forgetful, irrational, and nauseated, among other reactions. Roll with it all, and try to stay as focused as possible. Don't blame any slip-ups on being pregnant. Some of your colleagues are just waiting for you to admit it. You still have ultimate responsibility, and they don't deserve the satisfaction.

How to Keep Your Career Moving While Your Family Is Growing

An enlightened CEO is going to help you a lot, and even if you and your chief executive don't have a lot of contact, the trickle-down effect of family-friendly policies will benefit you. Look close to your level. Find somebody who's empathetic to your lifestyle.

- Don't be so anxious to climb the ladder that you take on more than what you can do well. Your mom duties are enormous, and if you can't handle it all right now, wait until you can. Don't set yourself up for failure.
- Have plenty of child-care coverage—and plenty of backup. Make sure you honor the schedule to which you've committed.
- When you're at work, be there to contribute. At the beginning, you're tempted to pick up the phone constantly to check on the baby. You learn what guilt is all about. Train yourself to turn it off.
- Don't go on and on about your children. People who talk about them incessantly, bringing their names into every conversation, drive others crazy.
- If you need an occasional extra hour in the morning or a day off because of obligations to your children, simply ask for the time. Don't give a long, detailed story about why you need it. A manager doesn't need to hear your personal business.
- Schedule the appointments of your children based on the needs of the business. Take one day off for all your routine pediatrician, dentist, and eye doctor appointments. If you keep leaving during the day, you're not perceived as someone who gives your job a lot of respect.
- If you're a manager, don't ask your staff to do something you would resent, such as staying late so that you can go home and be with your children.

BE APPRECIATIVE OF SPECIAL FAVORS

When Cyndi started her new job as marketing director, she was pregnant with her second child. She was worried because she knew that the CEO was intolerant of employees who didn't put work first. He became very ill, and during his long recovery he had an epiphany that changed the way he viewed the balance between work and family.

"He called me in the first day he was back," recalls Cyndi, "and asked me to head up a committee that would consider how we could make the company a better place for working mothers and fathers. He carries out his beliefs every day. I was sitting in a strategic planning meeting, and I knew I had to leave to pick up my children at day care. I didn't know how I could leave comfortably, but he must have seen me squirm. He said, 'If some of the people in the room have to leave because of family obligations, please feel free to go.' I sent him a note the next day thanking him for saving my credibility in front of my peers.

"But it goes even deeper. I got a call from a headhunter asking if I wanted to leave. I put him on hold, got back on, and told him, 'You could give me another ten thousand dollars, and I wouldn't leave. I'm staying here. I'm happy.' My CEO has my loyalty."

How to Be a Good Working Mother . . . at the Office

Remember that having children did not diminish your intelligence. Still, many women—especially those who have worked for the unenlightened or lunk-headed—have known for years that they have to work harder and be smarter in order to get ahead.

Keep the following in mind:

- Appreciate your strengths.

A research study published by Advanced Teamware, Inc., in 1995 found that women outperformed men in the softer skills of communicating, resolving conflicts, giving feedback, adapting to change, and motivating and inspiring others. Surprisingly, it showed that women also ranked higher than men in the traditional male skills of decisiveness, facilitating change, and planning. It's not a surprise to us women that women could do it, only that the majority of respondents recognized it.

- Keep emotion out of the situation.
  When you confront a problem, take a couple of days to think about your answer, until you're in control of your emotions. You don't have the time or energy to expend your energy wastefully.

- Understand that you're breaking ground, and live up to it.
  The last several people who held your position could have been men who were at least ten years older than you. Base your behavior accordingly. Plan before you write a report, present a presentation, or give direction. Know exactly what you intend to accomplish.

- Take advantage of a mentoring program.
  If there's not one in place, talk to someone you respect who's at a higher level who would be willing to talk with you about your career.

The Corporate Move (with Children)

There's only one good thing about a corporate move with a family: you don't have to find the mover or pack the boxes yourself. Moving is one of the great nightmares of life. It wasn't so bad when it was just you or just two of you, but factor in children, their five billion belongings, and friends that they can't possibly live without, and you have the components for potential disaster.

At last, corporations recognize the stress that relocating puts on a family. The corporate relocation department will help you deal with your child's day care, school, and little league needs, and a spouse's job search. If these services aren't available, ask your moving company. All the big ones have them.

MAKING YOUR MOVE GO SMOOTHLY

- Wait as long as possible to tell your children. Don't present them with a traumatic hypothetical situation and give them months to think about it.
- Use the resources from the moving company or corporate affairs department.

  They have consultants who specialize in easing your transition. Their predeparture training programs provide support for adjustment, as well as maps, information on schools, day care, real estate agents, contractors, and potential employers. They can direct you to someone in the new area to answer your questions. They also have special materials for your children, from kid-size colorful boxes to stickers to new address cards for old friends. Look for the "Relocation Journal" on the Internet.

- If you can, travel to the new destination to get your home and schools in place. Be able to reassure your children as much as possible.
- When you arrive, unpack and set up your children's rooms and playroom first. Be superhuman in your unpacking speed to make their transition as painless as you can.
- Put your own needs on hold for a while. When you move, you can be sure that someone in your family will be going through a crisis on any given day. You have to be the rock to help them adjust. After a while you'll be able to concentrate more on your own traumas. Until you feel the others are comfortable, don't indulge.

Your Best Strategy in the Workforce: Teach Other Women to Be Good Working Mothers

There are no classes or training for being a working mother. The only way to learn is woman-to-woman. We are one another's experts.

- Support other women in your company.
- Do whatever you can to make your office a positive place for working mothers.
- Start a lunchtime group that gets together once a month to discuss the issues and vent without fear of reproach.
- Seek other women to mentor.
- Take a working mother aside who looks as though she needs some friendly guidance.

And always remember how you're connected. Those little people at home are all your children, and the women in the workforce are your sisters.

▪ 12 ▪

Finding the Time to Give Back to Yourself

Shelly looks enviably calm sitting on a sofa in her corner office. While the snow has swirled and spun outside her window, and her assistant has fielded a trillion phone calls in the next room, she's just spent the last hour talking about how she organizes her life and enjoys her three children, how her family adapts to her career, and how she takes everybody to get haircuts and to the pediatrician. Though she gives me no indication she wants me to hurry out, I begin to pack up and thank her, but she leans forward and clasps her hands over her knee as if she wants to tell me one more story, to leave me with one more bit of inspiration.

"I went to a large breakfast meeting of professional women," she begins, "at which a woman who had just been appointed president of her company was honored. She got up to speak and said, 'I want to tell you what I did this year. I became president of my company, I relocated my mother to a retirement facility, I sold my mother's house, I moved my own family, I sold my house, I sent one of my children to college, I served on two boards, and I went to work every day. You know how I feel?'" Shelly pauses before the punch line. "'I'm so tired.'"

Shelly smiles as she tells me, "Every woman in that room got to her feet and applauded."

I can't get the image and the message out of my head as I venture back into the snowstorm and make my way through the slick streets. Our universal language is sleep deprivation. And self-deprivation.

As we try to make sense out of the world for everyone else, as we run through the blizzard of tasks, duties, obligations, and responsibilities on our lists, we seem to have left off one thing: us.

We understand very well what is important: our families. But as we make sure that they have everything they need to keep their lives runnning smoothly, we barely accommodate our own needs.

Do you go to the gym? Do you eat a proper lunch? Do you get your hair cut when you need it, or when you're desperate? When do you shop for *your* clothes? What's the last book you read in a reasonable amount of time? Do you ever go to a museum and see something besides dinosaur bones?

How are you going to have anything left to give your children?

Chill Out and Rethink Your Choices

"'Stress' is my password on my computer," says Marlene. What a watchword. Try peace or flower or mountaintop. Encourage the positive thoughts. Not that it's so easy. You're carrying a huge backpack of burden every day: the welfare and happiness of your family.

Every little shift in your mood, any offhanded remark you make, is imbued with tremendous power to affect the day of every person living in your house. It's no wonder we feel guilty.

WHAT'S IMPORTANT?

Brenda realized it had reached a critical point when she got a call one day at the office from her preschool son's nanny. "'They're putting the cast on now,' she told me, and I was shocked," recalls Brenda. "The night before, my son had told me that he'd hurt his leg at the playground and that he was having trouble walking, but I dismissed it and casually told the nanny to take him to the pediatrician. His leg was broken. If I had taken the time to recognize what was going on, I never would have done it like that. I would have taken him myself. It was completely inappropriate, and the amazing thing is that my son didn't know it was inappropriate." Is this what happens to us when we have no time to pause and listen?

We need to stop and fill ourselves back up—not to keep topping off our physical and emotional reservoirs with only a bit of sleep and a manicure every couple of weeks. And it takes a few seconds.

Take Care of Yourself Without Taking Any Extra Time

- Drop the need for perfection in one place. If you insist on a spotless house, for example, let one room go.
- Delegate one responsibility either at work or at home. It's a good feeling, and you'll find you might be able to do more.
- If you commute by public transportation, don't do any work on the ride home. Read a book instead.
- Use the first ten minutes of your commute to vent to yourself about your day. Try not to bring it home. Put yourself on a vitamin regimen, and be faithful about it. Ask for advice at the health food store, find it in a book, or consult a nutritionist.

- Have a cup of herbal tea in the evening. By yourself is great—or share the time with your husband or one child at a time.
- Drink those eight glasses of water a day you know you should be drinking.
- Indulge in really nice shampoos, soaps, and creams that make you feel pampered.
- Stop mothering the people at the office. They are adults and should be able to think for themselves. If they can't, there are solutions.
- Every day, look at something in nature: a flower, a blade of grass, trees, a bug, a pond, a sunrise, a sunset, the moon. It helps you keep it all in perspective.
- Don't be all things to all people.

IT WAS ALMOST TOO LATE

Marianne waited until she had to be hospitalized before she changed her ways. "I've set everybody's expectations a lot lower, and now they've stopped asking me or expecting me to do everything. I was going beyond a reasonable level. So now if I have to plan a birthday party and sell the house and pack up the house, I do one thing at a time. I set aside a little time during my lunch hour when I make the two phone calls I allow myself about whatever it is I'm working on."

She's also changed the way she eats lunch. She used to gulp yogurt and granola every day, but a nutritionist cautioned her that she needed real nutrition to regulate her energy levels. "My eating is much more holistic. I can still eat at my desk, but now I choose protein, carbohydrates, vegetables, fruit. It can be as thrilling as a turkey sandwich with lettuce and some juice, but I make sure I have it."

What to Do When You Schedule Some Time

EXERCISE

Nobody works out if it's left up to chance. You can think of a billion excuses, from not wanting to exercise next to a twenty-five-year-old in a tank top who climbs a Stairmaster for forty-five minutes at the highest level to having no discipline, energy, or time.

Working out gives you more energy, helps you lose weight, improves your circulation, tones your muscles, and makes you healthier. What's more, you have years and years ahead of you—nothing makes you more aware of your own mortality than your children—and you owe it to those who count on you to stay as healthy and vital as you can. Not everything is in your control, but exercise is.

GET UP AN HOUR EARLIER, AND ENJOY THE QUIET

Steal an hour to have coffee in your robe, read the paper or a book or a magazine or do a crossword puzzle, knit a sweater, or crochet a baby blanket.

GO FOR SOME BODYWORK

Massage, shiatsu, reflexology, facial, manicure, pedicure, waxing, aromatherapy.

TAKE A MENTAL HEALTH DAY

Schedule it around your birthday so that you're sure to do it every year. Go out for lunch with a good friend. Go shopping together. Take a tennis or golf lesson. Go to a jewelry store and try on things you would never buy. Throw a luncheon for three good friends. Sign up for a day of beauty at a salon. Go to an art gallery or museum. Browse through a bookstore all by yourself, and don't go near the children's section. Go to hear a speaker whose thoughts you admire.

So Why Are You Doing All This, Anyway?

Going to work, liking it, and doing well at it give you satisfaction that can't be discounted. You can feel successful in many ways at work, from proving what you'd set out to do in your career, to being proud of keeping everything cooking on four burners, to giving yourself permission to dream big. Some women who can't find the satisfaction at home in crippling marriages are validated only when they can go to work and prove their worth every single day, and then pick up a paycheck at the end of the week.

Others who also care for aging parents are relieved when they can deal with the beginning, middle, and end of each business day. You can feel proud to be giving your children a good look at a work ethic. Your success gives you the courage to trust your instincts and your talents.

Live Your Own Truth

In the best of all possible worlds, would you stay home with your children or would you go to work? And if you did go to work, would you work full-time or part-time? Well, if I've learned one thing by being a working mother and talking to hundreds more, it's that there's more than one way to be a good mother. We're really doing the best we can. If this book has helped you learn how to get a little bit more done, given you another idea about how to find a baby-sitter, or been the inspiration to give another working mother a helping hand, that's all you need.

Because by now you know that life isn't really about getting rid of dust bunnies, it's about making sure your own little bunnies are growing up into good people whom you're proud to call your own.

I wish you lots of luck, too, because as smart as we are, we all still need it.